Princess, Countess, Socialite, Spy

True Stories of High-Society Ladies
Turned WWII Spies.

Elise Baker

Table of Contents

Introduction

History has always been told by men and about men. The stories of male warriors, adventurers, and heroes are readily available and eagerly written by those interested in history. Unfortunately, this has left out a group of people integral to every success story. These people aided the wounded, carried and kept important information, and helped end wars. Take, for instance, the Second World War, the focus of this book. Many of us are familiar with the well-publicized stories of people such as Audie Murphy (who falsified his records), Georg Ferdinand Durkwitz (a German soldier who saved thousands of Jewish lives), and Oskar Schindler (who used his fortunes to save 1,200 Jewish people). These people have done great things; there is no negating this.

But where are the true stories of the women heroes of World War II? Where is the recognition of the part they played? Why have they been forgotten? Many people have become tired of reading about World War II and finding few accounts of female heroes. Brave male heroes are regularly celebrated, praised, honored, and written about, while their female counterparts are left behind. Women are far too often left out of the narrative. They are removed, made invisible, or have their contributions minimized.

Many true stories of espionage during World War II began to emerge with the declassification of secret military documents. This book shines a spotlight on the unique role played by high-society ladies, wives of high-status officials and wealthy, high-class women who risked their lives to aid the Allies by collecting valuable information, uncovering precious secrets and supplying Resistance movements. We will dig through the history of the Second World War and bring these true stories of female heroes to light. A tragic fact is this; many of these fearless women's stories were never truly told. The extent of their praise and admiration sometimes lies in a single sentence or is relegated to a few words in a report written up by men who believed that women should not be allowed to do the same work as men.

Espionage played a significant role in World War II. The Special Operations Executive (SEO) was a British organization serving during the Second World War. Their purpose was to sabotage, conduct espionage and reconnaissance in occupied Europe, and aid and arm Resistance groups against Nazi-occupied countries. It is true that this world *was and is* very secretive, but so many brave female spies in WWII have been forgotten. When they are remembered, their contributions and achievements are downplayed - made to seem small and unimportant to the greater cause. The few, rarely detailed, accounts that exist tend to focus on very superficial aspects of the female agents. The emphasis is placed on their femininity, physical appearance, powers of seduction, and female charm. These courageous women had varied international backgrounds. Almost all of them had extensive knowledge of various languages, some even polyglots. One would think that their multinational origins would make them unlikely candidates to be patriotic to a particular country, not necessarily their own, but they were often driven by passionate idealism; a burning desire to defend the values of freedom and liberty from the forces of oppression and occupation.

The remarkable women spies in World War II deserve to be celebrated for helping to achieve an Allied victory. After the victory, female agents were cast aside and not assigned the recognition they deserved. Where their male colleagues received military honors, which came with many benefits, including pensions, female agents were usually only awarded a civil honor. A significant redress of balance is long overdue in the field of espionage through history.

So, read on and join this adventure if you want to know why a few brave high-society ladies were attracted to Winston Churchill's call to "set Europe ablaze." Become immersed in the lives of five high-profile women who were drawn to the underground work of secret services during World War II. Learn more about the women who actively sought out these roles and those who were recruited to join the cause. Alongside this, gain an understanding of these organizations and their role in the war. And maybe, when all is said and done, you will feel inspired to dig deeper into the secret world of women in espionage during the Second World War.

Chapter 1:

The Baltimore Socialite – Virginia Hall

Also known as "The Limping Lady," the wonderful Virginia Hall is the first special agent whose story will be uncovered. She was a wonderful woman, a brave spy, and serves as a great example that you should never let anything stand in your way. Follow the tale of the woman some knew as "the most dangerous Allied spy."

A Life Before Espionage

Virginia Hall was born in Baltimore, Maryland, in 1906, 33 years before the onset of the Second World War. Born into a relatively wealthy family, Hall had her family's support in her studies and later travels. As a young lady at Columbia University (then Barnard College), she studied Italian, German and French. She wished to continue her studies in Europe and soon set off to travel through the continent. While in Europe, Hall studied in Austria, Germany, and France and eventually landed a job as a consultant service clerk at the United States Embassy in Warsaw, Poland. Hall set out to Europe, intending to work in the diplomatic corps.

However, an accident, which will be discussed in detail later, meant that her career as a diplomat might have ended before it could even begin. She transferred to a U.S. embassy from Warsaw in what is now known as Izmir, Turkey. After her accident, Hall continued to work as a consular clerk in both Venice and Tallinn, Estonia. But Virginia Hall was nothing if not resolute and persistent. Before the beginning of World War II, Hall made several attempts to work for the United States Foreign Service as a diplomat. But, not surprising for the times, women were rarely hired, and the difficulties she was left with after her injury meant that Hall was denied time and time again.

In 1939, she was turned down again; this time, the reason was linked to an obscure ableist rule (ableist referring to the unfair discrimination against those with physical or mental disabilities). Despite appealing to the then U.S. president, Franklin Roosevelt, she was still rejected. This rejection by Roosevelt felt quite ironic, as the president was confined to a wheelchair himself and had to overcome many difficulties and much prejudice to achieve his ambitions. Seemingly barred from following her dreams by the men surrounding her, Virginia Hall resigned from the Department of State in 1939. There are conflicting reports on what Hall did after this rejection. Some say she returned to America and attended graduate school in Washington D.C., while most report she moved from Estonia to France hoping for something greater. Regardless of the obstacles she faced, the story of the great spy Virginia Hall is far from over with this return home.

The Accident

For a moment, let us travel back in time to a few years before 1939 and the onset of World War II, and the start of Hall's espionage career. There is a key question that needs to be asked; Why is Virginia Hall known as "The Limping Lady?" While this might seem like a brilliant codename for a secret agent, the circumstances surrounding the origin of this name were less than ideal for Hall and her career as a diplomat for the Foreign Service.

In December of 1933, six years before the devastating outbreak of another world war, Hall was out hunting birds - a practice that wealthier families often participated in. Unfortunately, what transpired during this hunting session was anything but expected. Hall accidentally misfired her shotgun while climbing over a fence, doing irreversible damage to her left foot in a terrible twist of fate. By the time she was able to reach a hospital, gangrene had already set in. Her left leg was amputated below the knee, and she was fitted with a wooden prosthetic. It is widely known that she gave the wooden appendage the affectionate nickname 'Cuthbert'.

However, as is to be expected, the loss of part of her leg made walking an arduous task. One can only imagine that being fitted with a custom wooden leg (medical technology not being as advanced in 1933 as it is in modern times), was far more painful than it would be today. The prosthetic was attached to her body with a leather strap. This would not present any major problems for short distances in mild weather. But when working in hot weather and walking a lot, the leather would chafe the skin raw, and the stump would blister and bleed. In addition, climbing up and down was very difficult; the wooden ankle would not work as a normal ankle does, making Hall very vulnerable to falling. All of this makes some of her feats all the more incredible.

The adjustment of learning to walk with an uncomfortable wooden appendage explains why she was later known to the Gestapo as 'the Limping Lady.' Prior to the accident, Hall's hope of becoming a diplomat was improbable but not impossible; after the accident, it seemed to Hall that all hope was lost. Not only was she a woman wanting to work in a world dominated by men, but she was now also a disabled woman. For most, this might mean the end of all their hopes and dreams, but not for Miss Hall.

An Ambitious Woman in the World of Men

Before becoming a loved and loathed spy during the Second World War, Hall struggled to be taken seriously in her ambitions and pursuits. She spent several years working as a consular clerk at U.S. Embassies and Consulates while working to become a diplomat for the U.S. Foreign Service. In both December 1929 and July 1930, Hall failed to pass the difficult U.S. Foreign Service Exam. There was some speculation and rumors that after one attempt at the exam, her exam papers were mysteriously misplaced. After the second failed exam, she decided to travel overseas to gain some practical experience by working at United States Embassies and Consulates.

In September of 1934, Virginia Hall felt ready to return to work. Once used to walking with her prosthetic limb, she sent a request to the U.S. Department of State to be reinstated. Along with her request for reinstatement, she had a list of consulates she would prefer to work at. Unfortunately, none of her top choices had positions available. Instead, Hall was offered a position at the U.S. Consulate in Venice. A year after her unfortunate accident, in December 1934, she was back at work.

While working in Venice, Hall continued to pursue her dream of working for the U.S. Foreign Service. But once again, the odds were not in her favor. Although it might have been difficult to try and achieve her dreams prior to her accident, her being an amputee made it even more so. When she was still stationed at the embassy in Warsaw, Hall had begun the process of attempting to retake the U.S. Foreign Service exam for the third time; a process she continued to pursue in 1937. As a woman, working for the Foreign Services was an extremely competitive field to try and become a part of. At this time, only six in 1,500 Service officers were women, and these women had to adhere to some very stringent protocols. For example, a female Service officer had to be unmarried and would need to remain unmarried to continue working for the U.S. Foreign Service. If a female officer were to be married, regulations dictated that she resign from her commission.

Despite all her effort, Hall was rejected once again. This time the amputation of her leg served as cause for her rejection. The department at the time stated that all applicants had to be able-bodied. Under these regulations, Hall would not even be considered for the Foreign Service. Rightfully shocked by this, she attempted to appeal the decision. While awaiting the result of this appeal, Hall thought that perhaps a change of location would do her good. As a result, she accepted an open position at the U.S. Legation in Tallinn. She arrived in Tallinn in June 1938, where she continued to work as a consular clerk. In Tallinn, Hall sent her final appeal to the Assistant Secretary of State; she requested a waiver to retake the Foreign Service exam. Virginia Hall was turned down for a final time. After this rejection, she resigned from the U.S. Foreign Service and left for Paris in May of 1939. Hall did so, hoping she would find something greater, hoping she would find a cause she could contribute to and where she could reach her full potential.

Virginia Hall: Finally Recruited

Hall spent the summer of 1939 trying to decide what to do next. Finally, she received an answer to her problem; on September 1, 1939, Hitler invaded Poland. France, the country Hall found herself in at that time, declared war on Germany two days later. And so, Hall found her opportunity to help others. As a private, she enlisted in the French ambulance corps, known as the *"Services Sanitaires de l'Armée"*. During the time, which some refer to as the "Phony War" (September 1939 - May 1940), France and Germany engaged in minor scrimmages. While this took place, Hall received first aid training and began to work as an ambulance driver. She was now in the middle of the action and helping others, as she wanted to be, but it was challenging to drive with a wooden leg, and evacuating casualties from the front line was a dangerous task. Hall frequently had to drive down roads destroyed by fighter planes with machine guns.

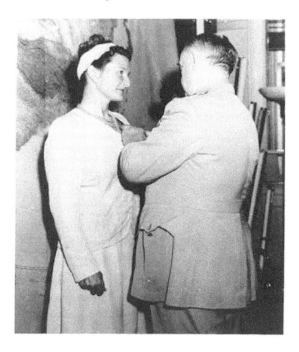

Figure 1: Virginia Hall of Special Operations Branch receiving the Distinguished Service Cross from General Donovan, September 1945. Photo courtesy of CIA.

From May 10, 1940, until June 14, 1940, Hall continued to work around the clock to help with the war effort by getting the wounded to safety. Then, on June 14th, 1940, Paris fell to German hands. Hall, a hopeful but inexperienced diplomat and a U.S. citizen, was stuck in occupied France. She was disgusted by the Nazi regime and their treatment of European Jews but was stuck in France, and she could not do anything to help. Soon she realized the only way to continue fighting against this terrible regime would be to go to England.

Via neutral Spain, Hall traveled to London in 1940. Before reaching London, and while still in Spain, she met a British Intelligence Officer named George Bellows. He sensed something about her, something that spoke of what an excellent agent she would make. Bellows later helped Hall secure a meeting in London with the British Special Operations Executive (SOE). In London, she checked into the U.S. Embassy and was immediately asked to debrief staff on the circumstances in occupied France. Despite all that Hall had done for the cause already, in September of 1940, she was hired by the U.S. Defense Attaché's Office. One can only imagine Hall's disappointment at this; she did not want to end up where she started. However, after surviving multiple bombings in London and the Battle of Britain, she was more determined than ever to get back in the field; she wanted to take the war to the Germans. In February 1941, Hall resigned from her job at the U.S. Embassy. The reason she stated for leaving was that she was "seeking other employment." The truth, however, was that she had been recruited by the British Special Operations Executive (SOE). The SOE was a secret British organization that operated during the Second World War. It was officially formed on 22 July 1940 by Winston Churchill and sometimes known as 'The Ministry for Ungentlemanly Warfare'. Its purpose was to conduct reconnaissance and sabotage missions against the Axis powers. They employed more than 13,000 people, and about 3,200 of those were women. The SOE officially disbanded in January 1946.

She was an ideal agent; she had received an extensive education, was fluent in French, German, and Italian, and had already spent some time on the frontlines. Hall completed the SOE's rigorous and demanding training program and became an agent in April 1941. Summer that year was spent planning her deployment in Vichy France. Throughout her career as a spy, Hall operated under many codenames (which meant that information about her and her missions were often unattainable); the codename used during this mission was 'Germaine.' She arrived in France in August 1941, assuming the cover (which held the truth) of a French-speaking American reporter working for the New York Post.

During this time, agents were usually kept in the field for no longer than six months. Hall, however, stayed in Lyon for 15 months. She was the first female agent recruited by the SOE and the only agent to operate in France for well over a year. Interestingly, the deployment of more women agents was mainly due to her success. She was arming, funding, supplying, and organizing the French Resistance. Hall did many important things during her time in Lyon. She rescued Allied airmen who were shot down and ensured their safe return to London; she oversaw parachute drops that provided resources to Resistance fighters. In addition, Hall organized attacks sabotaging German supply lines. Hall was doing everything she possibly could to help. Hall had a sixth sense which alerted her to any potential danger. Her extreme caution was one of the reasons she managed to remain as long in the field as she did, despite the odds that were always against her. M.R.D. Foot, the official historian of the SOE, remarked that she truly lived by the motto of every successful secret agent: *Dubito, ergo sum* (I doubt, therefore I survive). Despite her caution, her successes drew the attention of the French Vichy Police and the German Gestapo. She had to flee and, after much struggle, returned to London to be greeted by her colleagues as a hero. Hall completed a few more undercover missions for the SOE; however, the organization refused to send her back behind German lines because she was still actively being hunted by the Gestapo across France. As a result, Hall joined the U.S. equivalent of the SOE in March 1944. This organization was known as the U.S. Office of Strategic Services (OSS).

The OSS was the United States' intelligence agency during World War II. The agency's purpose was to conduct espionage behind enemy lines for all branches of the U.S. Armed Forces. After the attack on Pearl Harbor, which resulted in the United States joining the war effort, the OSS became far more involved and urgent in their actions. The organization disbanded a month after the end of the war. However, Hall was still not given seniority, and could only enter France on her new mission as an assistant to a less experienced male colleague. She was now codenamed 'Diane' and entered France in the disguise of a shuffling, elderly peasant woman, which provided a convincing cover for her limp. She posed as an ageing cook on a farm, where taking the cows out to pasture gave her an opportunity to scout for fields suitable for agents and supplies to be dropped in. She and the other agent landed at the coast of Bretagne, in a rubber boat, under cover of darkness. They set up operations in Maidou - a village south of Paris. There they monitored and reported on German troop movements. In 1944, with the Allied invasion of France drawing closer, Hall was instructed to organize the local French Resistance; after Lyon, this was nothing new to her, although still extremely difficult without officially being in a position of command.

So, Hall had been recruited. She had now worked for two espionage agencies during World War II, organized multiple Resistance causes, saved lives, and aided those on the front lines. But what happened after the war? Did she have a career? Was she as honored and praised as her male counterparts? With an incredible career such as hers, there are many unbelievable moments to pick from to describe her as a person and a spy; yet there are still a few that stand out among the others, and these stories will unfold in the next chapter.

Chapter 2:

The Limping Lady's Story Continues

Virginia Hall achieved many remarkable things during her time as a spy. She was loved and praised by her colleagues and loathed by those whose plans she foiled. Some of the things she had to do or endure during the war were incredible, only cementing her status as an admirable and brave woman. But the praise received during the war did not necessarily carry over to Hall's career after the war.

Three Key Moments in the Life of Virginia Hall

Virginia Hall was indeed an extraordinary spy. Despite her prosthetic leg, she evaded capture, saved fellow agents, and crossed dangerous mountains. Most people would instinctively seek to avoid exposure to risk and to hide from danger during wartime, yet Virginia Hall actively sought out both! She had fallen in love with France at a young age, and she could not abandon the country that meant so much to her.

The Unexecuted Wrath of Klaus Barbie

Virginia Hall visited the country of France when she was a young woman of around 20 years old. Paris left quite an impression on her. It was a great city of art and culture, freedom, and emancipation. Hall's experience there broadened her horizons to new things and feelings. Paris left such an imprint on Hall's heart and mind that she once stated that everything she did during the war was done for her love of France.

To see this incredible country fall into the hands of a group of terrible people made Hall even more determined to do all she could to help. While she was organizing the French Resistance in 1941, Hall drew the attention of the French Vichy Police and the Gestapo. Now being on their radar, the French gave her an interesting nickname that would later be applied by the Nazis as well; "La dame qui boite" (Purnell, 2019), or "the Lady with the Limp."

With the invasion of North Africa, the Nazis took complete control over France, and with this takeover came Klaus Barbie. Barbie was placed in charge of the Gestapo operating in former French Vichy areas. Barbie was notorious as a man who enjoyed torturing others. Like Hall, this notoriety gave him a nickname; "The Butcher of Lyon." Barbie did not take long to become obsessed with finding the elusive 'Germaine.' The Gestapo was never able to discover her true identity but had gathered enough intel to know they were looking for a French-Canadian woman (or so they thought). Barbie had placed a large bounty on Hall, offering money for any information that could lead to her arrest. Hall had heard much about Barbie's activities before assuming control of the Gestapo in France. He had a penchant for torturing Jews and French Resistance members and used particular methods on female prisoners. Knowing this makes Hall's refusal to back down all the more impressive. Barbie considered her the "enemy's most dangerous spy" (Purnell, 2019) and would do anything to capture her.

Because of this, when Barbie took over the Gestapo, he launched a nationwide hunt for Hall. He was so eager to capture her that he had hundreds of 'Wanted!' posters displayed in the streets all over France to gather information about her or find a way to flush her out. The Gestapo gave her the codename 'Artemis', and left no stone unturned in searching for the Lady with the Limp. But when Barbie reached Lyon, Virginia Hall was long gone, having crossed the Pyrenees. Sixteen months after her escape, he was still eager to find her. Barbie reportedly told his staff: "I would give anything to lay my hands on that Canadian bitch" (Purnell, 2019). Eventually, Klaus Barbie's luck would run out, and Allied forces would capture him. Sensing that he could be an asset, Barbie spent a few years working with various intelligence groups. Five years after Hall's death, he would have to stand trial for his crimes against humanity and Lyon. Barbie was found guilty and sentenced to life in prison. He died in 1991 - never having caught the "Canadian bitch" that made his job so difficult.

The Unbelievable Hike Across the Pyrenees

In November of 1942, Hall was informed that an Allied invasion of North Africa was nearing. She anticipated that the Abwehr (the German military intelligence service) and Gestapo's suppression would become more severe, and she would be correct. So, as Germany seized control of the entire country of France, Hall had to escape from France as soon as possible. Hall had communicated with those in London for quite some time, but every time they scheduled a date she could leave, she would receive another call to help someone. No matter the danger she faced, Hall could not leave knowing she could have saved someone from the clutches of the Gestapo. When it was simply too dangerous for Hall to remain in France any longer, she fled from Lyon by train to Perpignan, where she met with a guide who would assist and accompany her to Spain. With the invasion of North Africa, Hall knew that borders would be sealed and the men hunting her down her were hot on her heels. She escaped with hours to spare. But it is not this last-minute escape from France that astounded so many of Hall's colleagues and superiors. No, it was the journey The Limping Lady took to reach the safety of Spain.

The Pyrenees is a sizable mountain range forming a wall between France and Spain. In November, the temperatures in the lower elevation of the mountain range bordered on freezing, with the mountain pass covered in ice and snow. In two days, covering about 50 miles a day, and crossing a 7,500-foot pass, Hall and her guide hiked across the Pyrenees to reach Spain. This hike is no mean feat for any relatively fit and able-bodied human being. But Hall was anything but average. With her affectionately nicknamed wooden leg, Cuthbert, Hall traveled across the mountain range in the snow in two days. Because her wooden leg and ankle did not function as a normal leg would, one can only imagine that she would have to take one step and then brace herself swinging her left leg forward to progress. The relentless climbing and descent with her prosthetic leg magnified the danger Hall was in and the pain she must have experienced. At one point during their journey, in her communications with fellow SOE agents, Hall joked that she was doing fine, but 'Cuthbert' was giving her trouble. Not knowing that this was the name she had given to her prosthetic leg, SOE headquarters replied: "If Cuthbert is giving you difficulty, have him eliminated." The confusion resulted in a bit of humor, much needed during this time.

It is estimated that Hall and her guide reached the border of Spain on November 11, 1942. Unfortunately, in her rush to escape, Hall did not have the correct documentation to cross the border. As a result, she was imprisoned for 20 days for illegally crossing the Spanish border. Luckily, Hall was released and returned to London with the help of the U.S. Embassy. By late December, despite the danger she faced due to being on the Gestapo's most-wanted list, Hall was determined to return to France. However, as previously stated, the SOE refused her requests to return to France; they considered her cover to be blown and that it would be too dangerous to send her back while Barbie was still searching for her. So, for two months in 1943, she worked undercover in Madrid as a reporter for the *Chicago Tribune*. Hall's main task during her time in Madrid was setting up and running safe houses. Then in March 1944 she joined the OSS, who were willing and prepared to send her back behind enemy lines in France.

The Exceptional Mauzac Breakout

One of Hall's most praised missions during the war is the Mauzac jailbreak. It utilized all the skills she had gained, not only from training, but from spending so long in the field. Hall was the mastermind behind an escape plan designed to free 12 captured agents. Once all 12 agents were free and safely returned to London, the result showed just how cunning, intelligent and courageous Virginia Hall was.

In October 1941, 12 agents were captured and imprisoned. They were kept in the Perigueux Prison until later transferred to the internment camp at Mauzac. Due to the horrible conditions they were kept in, they were in fragile health, and if kept in the original prison for much longer, they would not have survived. Hall's initial plan to free her fellow agents was to aid them in escaping during their transfer between Perigueux and Mauzac. But, due to their weakened state, they would have been unable to run fast. Pair that with the armed guards escorting them and the outcome of an escape attempt at that time would have had terrible consequences.

Instead, Hall spent months hatching and implementing a plan to free the agents, now kept at Mauzac. The conditions in Mauzac were much better, and the men began regaining their strength. Her first order of business was finding a way to communicate with the agents. Hall herself could not physically visit them in prison; she was too well known and would be arrested before entering the grounds. Luckily, she was able to enlist the help of one of the agents' wives. Jean Pierre Bloch, a former French deputy, had heard of Virginia Hall and instructed his wife, Gaby Bloch, to meet with Hall in Lyon. From there, Gaby became an instrumental part in freeing the 12 men. Gaby would later be honored and recommended for the King's Medal for Courage in the Cause of Freedom.

With the help of Gaby, Hall smuggled tools and messages into the prison. She ensured Gaby had clean clothes, books and large quantities of groceries for each visit. Due to the frequency of Gaby's visits, she was often searched upon entering the camp. However, miraculously, the guards never discovered the tools that Hall and Gaby had hidden in some of the items; including a small file, a pair of wire cutters, and tins of sardines (these would later be used to fashion the key with which the agents escaped). Gaby also helped smuggle messages to the men in tubes of aspirin. Some 'friendly' guards, who will be mentioned again soon, helped transport these messages. The messages would be passed to a colleague who was in contact with Gaby during her visits; the tube would be placed inside his coat pocket, where he left it hanging. But one of these messages was misdelivered; it mistakenly ended up in the jacket of the mess sergeant. On her next visit, Gaby was immediately called into his office and confronted with the escape plan. Luckily for Hall and everyone involved, the sergeant was willing to help them in exchange for 50,000 francs, which Hall swiftly provided.

Hall was quick to look for guards in Mauzac who might be sympathetic to the cause, and either willing to help or to turn a blind eye. The first guards Hall approached seemed interested, but it came to nothing. However, the last guard Hall befriended, Jose Sevilla, was willing to help. He had only one request; he wanted to be taken to London. One major aspect of the plan Sevilla helped with involved one of the watchtowers. He convinced the camp commander that watchtower five, the watchtower closest to the agents, should not be manned at night. Sevilla explained that the tower posed some safety issues; it tended to sway in the wind, making the ladder to the platform unsafe in the dark.

But it was not only wives, guards, and Hall that played significant roles in the escape. Georges Bégué, one of the imprisoned agents, helped prepare for the escape and the aftermath from within the prison. Bégué used the tools smuggled in by Gaby to create a copy of the key they would need to open where they were being kept. He used bread from the canteen to form a mold from the lock and then make a key. Unfortunately, his first attempt at making the key failed. The second attempt, luckily, was a success. Bégué was also a wireless operator and used a transmitter smuggled in by a French priest working with Hall to send messages to SOE agents in London.

From outside the prison, Hall displayed her training and organizational skills. She might not have been able to visit the prisoners herself, but she did not let that deter her from doing all she could to ensure their safety after the escape. Hall arranged safe houses and eventual passage over the Pyrenees using some of her regular contacts. She recruited a getaway driver and arranged for 12 sets of train tickets, ration cards, and false papers. Those involved in the escape knew that a chase would be inevitable once guards realized the men were gone. To combat this, Hall found a hideaway place close to the camp. There the men could stay safe for the first few days post-escape when the danger of being recaptured was highest.

So, with everything carefully planned and tested and with friendly guards on their side, the time came for the men to escape from the Mauzac internment camp. On the 15th of July 1942, a lit cigarette on watchtower seven at three a.m. signaled that the time had come. The key turned in the lock this time, and the men ran to the fence and began crawling out from under the wire, only once encountering a friendly guard who warned them they were being too loud. In 12 minutes, 12 men escaped. They were safely guided away by the bribed mess sergeant and ran quietly into the night. Their absence was only discovered at dawn, and a subsequent search failed to find the escaped agents; they were safe.

In the aftermath, Hall proved that she did indeed think of everything. She ensured Gaby would have a concrete alibi for when she was, inevitably, arrested after the escape; a witness was produced, who was prepared to confirm that Gaby could not have been involved. Hall deliberately circulated rumors about how the men could have escaped, and with no way of proving which rumors held substance, there was no way to find the men. All 12 men eventually made it safely to London. Hall had pulled off a spectacular prison break that would be discussed with admiration for years to come. Virginia Hall never took credit for this escape; in fact, several other agents pretended it was their own master plan. However, this would always be a mission attributed to her skills and dedication.

Highest Honors

Sadly, Hall did not receive the honors and recognition she deserved. Although we wish that more people knew about her activities and talent, she was not unduly bothered by the lack of attention. To Hall, what she was doing was not for the medals, ceremonies, or decorations. She kept very quiet about what she accomplished. Instead, she believed it was all about doing your duty, earning respect from those you work with, and excelling in your job.

Hall received some recognition during the war, even if not all the attempts to honor her panned out. After her work in Lyon and the escape from Mauzac, the SOE volunteered Hall for a CBE (Commander of the Order of the British Empire), the highest award the British could present to a civilian. An internal SOE F-Section memo states, "Many of our men owe their liberty and even their lives to Virginia Hall" (Purnell, 2019). She was not awarded the CBE. But a year later, in 1943, Hall was awarded an MBE (Member of the Order of the British Empire) with no public announcement or ceremony, as Hall was still active in the field and could not risk being uncovered.

The British were not the only ones to recognize Hall's excellence. She received the Croix de Guerre for her unwavering service to France. However, the French were quite slow to recognize her role in their liberation. In 2006, President Jacques Chirac honored her for the first time as a "true hero of the French Resistance." After the war, Hall received the Distinguished Service Cross, given by the OSS for extraordinary heroism. She was the only civilian woman to receive this award. Despite many wanting it to be a big ceremony, Hall insisted on a small, private ceremony. This insistence was, in part, because she wanted to continue working as a secret agent so she could not have any publicity about her role in espionage during the war. In 1945, in Washington D.C. General William Donavan presented Hall with her award. After her death in 1988, Hall was inducted into the Military Intelligence Corps Hall of Fame. In addition, the CIA publicly acknowledged her work, citing her in the catalog of the OSS in the CIA Museum and named a training building after her.

Life After War

Hall's life after the war *began* during the Second World War. While working for the OSS, Hall met Paul Goillot. Goillot was a fellow operative, a French-American lieutenant who lived in New York and Paris. He and Hall fell in love almost immediately. In September 1944, Hall was in charge of organizing a parachute drop as the war was winding down. One of the men taking part in this parachute drop was Goillot. Hall and Goillot began working together and, on September 14, both left Cosne to look for more German troops. By September 25, they had made it to liberated Paris. After the war, Hall returned to the U.S. and lived with Goillot in New York City. The couple would get married in the 1950s while both worked for the CIA. Paul Goillot was a breath of fresh air for Hall. Paul was shorter than her, seven years younger, and her junior in rank. He brought laughter back into her life after many years when laughter was scarce. As Sonia Purnell mentioned in her biography, *A Woman of No Importance* (2019); as a female agent with a license to kill and a leader of men who often treated her with hostility and disrespect, with abject fear as her constant companion, how wonderful it is that she found personal happiness after what she had endured. Her disability had also caused her isolation and loneliness, which she would not have to feel any longer now that she had Paul.

In 1945, Hall visited Lyon, hoping to learn the fate of some of those she worked with during the war. She was happy to learn that a handful of those she trusted and operated with survived but faced great sadness when she learned that most did not make it out of the war. Hall returned to the United States in September of 1945 but felt like a stranger in the country where she had spent most of her life. Coming home was not as filled with joy as she had hoped it would be. Like so many others who returned to a life of peace after a war, Hall took quite some time to adjust to a calmer life. Hall's reunion with her mother was also not what she had hoped for, though she asked her mother to accompany her when she received her award. Her mother still exerted a domineering influence over her daughter, that fearless leader of partisan fighters! She disapproved of Paul and opposed their relationship. Hall was 40 years old when she arrived back in the United States, childless and unmarried. She was never the society lady her mother had always wanted her to be. Hall learned to live with this, but it upset her at the time.

Like so many others who had played their part in World War II, Hall struggled to find a job after the OSS was disbanded. She was lucky enough to receive one final paycheck but was left to fend for herself after that. Goillot also struggled to find a job; like Hall, he could not disclose who his previous employer was, and he had no further education after high school. Hall struggled even more. She was a disabled woman with no way to tell a potential employer that she was a spy during the war. No number of medals or awards could help those returning from the war find a way to make a living and survive.

In March of 1946, Hall tried once more to join the U.S. Foreign Services after President Truman dissolved the OSS. This time, she was not rejected for her gender or disability but rather due to budget cuts; apparently, there was no money to take Hall onboard. So, in 1951, Virginia Hall joined the Central Intelligence Agency - then known as the Central Intelligence Group. President Truman created this intelligence group after tensions rose in the Soviet Union. Hall tried to find a job in the agency from the very beginning. Upon her return to the U.S., Hall worked in New York City in the division of the CIA called the National Committee for Free Europe.

Hall was one of the first women hired by the CIA and later became the first woman to become a member of the Career Staff in 1956. At first, she received some small missions abroad, but she was stuck behind a desk watching the men work in the front. Hall desperately wanted to stay in the field, to be out there where the action was, but despite her best efforts, she was relegated to desk work and used as an analyst. For

15 years, she used her expertise in various missions and activities. Hall's background knowledge was used to support Resistance groups operating in Iron Curtain countries. Little was known about Hall outside the field of intelligence agencies, and, after the war, she faced a lot of prejudice and misunderstanding in her career. She was shifted to the side by her superiors. Hall was resented by many of her male colleagues at the CIA; none had close to her level of experience in the field nor could match her heroic achievements during the war and perhaps this embarrassed them. Despite this, they still received higher pay and were given seniority over Hall. She was knowingly excluded repeatedly and belittled in her annual reviews. From the perspective of an outsider, or those that had the opportunity to work with Hall during the war, it was as if she was once again only a second-class citizen. Here, in an office far removed from the dangers of the frontline, she was just a woman. It seemed as if all the hard-won respect that Hall had gathered during the war dissipated once it had ended, she was nothing more than a nuisance to the men in charge. If war had thrown open the doors of opportunity to Hall and given her a chance to shine, those doors began to close again in peace time.

Hall was never bitter; she continued to do her best and perform her duties to the best of her abilities. When she reached the mandatory retirement age of 60, she left the agency and retired to a farm in Maryland, where she lived quietly with her husband Paul. In July 1982, Virginia Hall died at the age of 77. As Purnell (2019) stated in her writings about Hall, she did not receive the recognition she deserved from the CIA for her time working for them. Toward the end of her life, there were some indications that this was beginning to change and that her efforts were being acknowledged. In the 21st century, Virginia Hall is now recognized by the CIA as a true war hero. It is now known that her career was held back by superiors who did not know how to utilize her talents correctly. Virginia Hall is now one of only five agents and the only woman featured in the CIA museum catalog. Her career might not have begun and ended the way she hoped it would, but the difference she made in the field of intelligence and the role she played during World War II will never be forgotten.

Chapter 3:

The Polish Aristocrat –
Christine Granville

Born under one name and dying under another, Christine Granville played a significant part in Poland's military strategies during the Second World War. Granville is the second female spy whose story needs to be detailed. So, follow the story of a spy who deserved far more than life gave her.

The Life of Krystyna Skarbek

Figure 2: Krystyna Skarbek ©Imperial War Museum (HU 479520)

Born in Warsaw in 1908 as Maria Krystyna Janina Skarbek, known as Krystyna Skarbek. She was born into a family of highly patriotic aristocrats loyal to Poland, even though Poland would not be acknowledged as a country until she was ten years old. Her father was

Count Jerzy Skarbek, a Roman Catholic. Though descended from a wealthy family, he was in a tremendous amount of debt. However, all his problems would be solved when he married Stefania Goldfeder. Stefania was the daughter of a wealthy Jewish banker. Though the marriage benefitted both parties, no one would call their marriage a happy one. Jerzy continued to live his lavish lifestyle, which Stefania was not fond of.

The birth of their first child seemed, at first, to bring some positivity into their marriage. However, this did not last long as their son Andrzej grew older, and Jerzy realized he took after his wife more than he took after the Count. Luck would strike Jerzy when Krystyna grew into a young girl. She became very attached to her father and he to her. They both shared a sense of adventure and enjoyed being active. Krystyna immersed herself in sporting activities such as skiing and horseback riding from an early age. In her naïvety, she idolized and praised her father and could not understand why her mother seemed closed off and withdrawn.

In modern times, Krystyna would undoubtedly be described as a tomboy; she was active, mischievous, and did not behave in the way that girls of her social standing were expected to. Hoping to nudge her daughter in the direction that would shape her into a young lady, Stefania sent Krystyna to a boarding school. Krystyna was by no means unintelligent; on the contrary, she learned languages quickly and excelled in her subjects at school. But she always wanted to push against the rules. This attitude led to her being dismissed from the first boarding school. She soon realized that, despite the dismissal, she would not be returning home and chose to focus on her studies instead. She soon became a top student fluent in multiple languages. However, her time at the boarding school was not always happy. The girls she attended school with came from prestigious families and looked down on Krystyna because of her Jewish mother. This bigotry would not be the first time Krystyna felt excluded due to her half-Jewish heritage.

In 1926, Poland was suffering from the economic depression following World War I. Like many others, the Skarbek family was hurt financially by this time, so they had to auction off some of their possessions. One could speculate that this was the beginning of a shift in Krystyna's perspective of the world. When Poland was invaded in the Second World War, she would face an assault on her innocent memory of a perfect Poland, of freedom.

At the age of 21, Krystyna joined her mother and brother in living in an apartment in Warsaw. Her father had not ceased his extravagant lifestyle, and she had to face some harsh realities. Krystyna had to accept that her father was not the man she believed him to be; he had abandoned her mother, become an alcoholic and was increasingly anti-Semitic. Count Jerzy Skarbek died in December of 1930 of tuberculosis (TB) near Vienna. Despite their financial difficulties, no cost was spared when organizing his funeral. His body was returned to Poland, and he was buried in the family plot.

Krystyna received an education, but it did not prepare her for more than being a society wife; at this point, Krystyna's prospects looked bleak. Her family's half-Jewish roots and new poverty reduced her chances of finding a good marriage. As she still had the right to use the Skarbek name, Krystyna was invited to many society parties. Unfortunately, the 21-year-old never enjoyed these parties. The older society women gossiped about her family's misfortune and judged her for her Jewish blood.

In a lively and social Poland, Krystyna enjoyed her freedom, but she was unwilling to be a burden on her mother. To earn some money of her own, she started an office job at a Fiat dealership in the capital. For the adventurous Krystyna, this office job offered nothing but tedium. Along with the boredom came some health issues. Exhaust fumes were slowly poisoning her from the workshop underneath the office. The fumes left permanent dark spots on her lungs (that would later come in handy), and doctors advised her to take to nature and let the clear air heal her lungs.

At this job, she met her first husband, Gustav Gettlich. Both enjoyed skiing and thus spent a good portion of their relationship before their marriage skiing in Zakopane. However, despite her blossoming relationship with Gettlich, Krystyna was still heavily ostracized by the society ladies for her part-Jewishness. In Zakopane, Krystyna could not remain as anonymous as she could in Warsaw. So, despite her ever-growing skills as a skier, Krystyna did not feel free to be herself even in a place she held dear.

Back in Warsaw, Gettlich and Krystyna continued to spend their free time together. Her time in Zakopane and being the subject of malicious and judgmental gossip had, however, negatively affected her self-esteem. Krystyna desperately wanted to regain some of her lost pride, so in 1930 she entered a beauty competition. Four weeks after entering the competition, she learned that she had been shortlisted. The competition's acknowledgment of her beauty confirmed to Gettlich that she was a good catch and would make a beautiful bride. This acknowledgment is the first time noted by historians that her beauty overshadowed her accomplishments - something that would occur time and again in her career as a spy. In April 1930, Krystyna and Gettlich got married in a small wedding. At this time, Gettlich was a wealthy but untitled 25-year-old, clearly infatuated with Krystyna, and she was an ambitious 21-year-old who had been marginalized and recognized only for her beauty. Krystyna was all too relieved by the marriage and the pending financial security.

Although Krystyna might have the financially stable life her mother had always wanted for her, Gettlich did not have the submissive housewife he thought he was getting. Krystyna continued to go to bars, ski, and have the kind of fun that was inappropriate for a wife during this era. She also gained skills that would prove helpful to her in her later espionage career. To feel some excitement, she began smuggling cigarettes past border patrols across the peaks of Poland and, in doing so, came to know some secret mountain paths. Sooner rather than later, the couple acknowledged that neither was happy in the marriage, so in 1932 they got divorced.

Divorced, poor, and half-Jewish, Krystyna Skarbek felt like she had no social status left to lose. While this did give her more freedom, it in no way lessened the gossip spread by older society ladies. While Krystyna was enjoying her newfound freedom, she met the man who would become her second husband, Jerzy Giżycki. Giżycki was quite a few years older than Krystyna but by no means less adventurous. Many believe that drew them to each other; both had a longing to see the world and be active for as long as they could. He was the only man, besides maybe her father, whose sense of adventure matched her own.

Krystyna and Jerzy were an extremely charismatic couple, but something was evident from the get-go; Krystyna's mood and confidence levels were greatly influenced by how Jerzy felt and behaved at any moment in time. When he felt comfortable in a social situation, she was confident and sociable; when he was irritated and anxious, she would become shy. When they grew restless in Warsaw and Poland, they traveled to various countries and surrounded themselves with diverse cultures and people. While traveling, Jerzy visited clubs and wrote books, and Krystyna showed her skills at skiing, perfected her French, and dabbled in journalism. By the time they married in November of 1938, their relationship was well-established and as full of excitement as when they met.

The couple were still in the midst of their travels when, at the end of 1938, the Polish Foreign Office called upon Jerzy. He was to serve his country as a senior diplomat and open a consulate in Kenya (though some sources suggest it could also have been Ethiopia). Krystyna was certainly not what people would describe as a traditional diplomat's wife. She was restless, unpredictable, and struggled with the idea of settling down; she could not be the quiet and submissive wife some expected her to be. But her beauty and determination would undoubtedly act as an asset. They headed off to London to complete some formalities. Her husband seemed to be in his element there, but Krystyna was anything but comfortable; the life of a diplomat's wife was not for her. After a few weeks, they boarded a steamship to South Africa. They would arrive in Cape Town and, from there, travel to Nairobi. Their travels through South Africa were not without some obstacles, but Krystyna was in *her* element. They reached Johannesburg in August of 1939 and, on September 1st, Hitler invaded Poland. Two days after the invasion, Britain would join France in declaring war on Germany. Over 5,000 miles away and unable to help from South Africa, Krystyna and her husband decided the only thing to do was to head back to Britain and help their country. It is here that Krystyna's life of espionage began.

Finally! A Life of Adventure

Despite only just arriving in Johannesburg, the couple set off for Cape Town once again in the hopes of finding a way to return to London. In Cape Town, Jerzy sold the car, and they managed to buy a passage on a ship to Southampton. Within two weeks of the initial invasion, Warsaw was surrounded. Britain had asked Poland to hold off on retaliating for another two weeks so the Allied forces could launch an attack. Instead, the British forces dropped thousands of useless propaganda pamphlets in German cities. Soon, Poland faced war on multiple fronts, and on September 28, 1939, the capital fell. All of this took place while Krystyna and Jerzy were on a ship, making many stops, slowly working their way to Southampton.

By the time they reached Britain in October of 1939, some estimated the Polish casualties to be around 200,000. Unfortunately, at this stage, neither of them could find out what had happened to their family members living in Poland. One thing was sure, though, as they headed to London, they might have missed the opportunity to enlist in the army in Poland, but they would not sit in Britain and watch the war happen. Jerzy would learn that he could not join the fight due to his age and some old injuries. But Krystyna would find a way to employ her skills and lust for adventure and danger to help her homeland.

Luckily, Krystyna knew exactly whom to talk to about joining the cause. Historians are divided about how Krystyna came to meet the necessary people; some believe it was through journalist Frederick Augustus Voight others believe it was through her husband's connections. Whatever the case may be, Krystyna managed to have a meeting with George Taylor. Taylor held a prominent position in Section D (or Section Destruction). Section D would later become the SOE, and most of its members would be brought up through the "old boys' network"; everyone knew everyone because they all grew up in the same high-society circles. Krystyna, not part of any "old boys' network," would be unable to join the organization in this way, so she simply demanded to be taken on.

Before arriving in Britain from South Africa, she had already devised a plan to volunteer to work as a spy. She had also already created a plan to help the Resistance in Poland. As expected, Krystyna was met with a great deal of skepticism. She was a Polish woman, half-Jewish; what use could she possibly be? Nevertheless, Krystyna persisted, and, eventually, the plan was approved. Krystyna Skarbek and her regular life would be left behind in Britain, and her life as an intelligence agent in the Second World War would begin.

Chapter 4:

The Queen of the European Underground is Born

Krystyna Skarbek left her life and name behind and became who we know today as Christine Granville. From surviving multiple close calls during the war to a life filled with struggle after, Granville remains one of the bravest women to work in espionage during World War II.

Defining Christine Granville in Three Momentous Moments

Skiing Into The Polish Underground

The British intelligence had hoped that they could support and fortify the underground Resistance in Poland and create some sort of guard against Germany. Christine Granville (at this stage still Krystyna Skarbek) showed them how they could reassure the people of Poland that they had not abandoned them. So, in December 1939, she assumed her first false identity, Madame Marchand. Granville left for Hungary on the 21st of December 1939. She flew from London to Paris and then boarded a train to Budapest.

Granville's transfer from London to the field happened quickly, with her clearance at MI5 (Military Intelligence, Section 5) only finalized in March of 1940. The Secret Intelligence Service (SIS) approved Granville's self-formed mission without full endorsement. Granville was sent out on a six-month trial period with the cover of working as a French journalist, some contacts in Budapest, £250, and some basic instructions on explosives. She arrived in Budapest three months after Poland was invaded. It would go on record to be one of the coldest winters ever, so she hurried to the apartment arranged for her stay in Derék Utca. It was a small apartment, but Granville quickly settled and was ready to carry out her mission. It is important to note that despite the Hungarian-Polish friendship, the small country could not afford to upset Hitler and thus remained a neutral territory.

Her first point of contact was Hubert Harrison, a correspondent for the *News Chronicle*, who worked for George Taylor. However, the pair struggled to work together from the start. Harrison was supposed to provide Granville with training, technical support, and further contacts, and in return, she would provide a link to the Polish people. With their association came other issues; the Polish intelligence in Budapest had already been keeping an eye on Harrison and could now add Granville to their list.

Her second point of contact was a journalist friend from Poland, Józef Radzimiński - his extreme infatuation with Granville would prove to be quite problematic later when he drew unnecessary attention to them both with lovesick theatrics. For now, he introduced her to several other journalists and diplomats. But she soon grew tired of his constant presence and was able to, on her own, quickly learn different signals and how to spot them, making her life more manageable and somewhat safer. Luckily for Granville, several foreign journalists traveled to the free countries closest to the action in Europe, and a good number of those were women. Her cover as a French journalist was thus wholly believable, and her frequent movements were not deemed strange.

Hungary kept its borders open for Polish and military refugees, and, as such, Granville met a childhood friend, Andrzej Kowerski. He was a lieutenant and as drawn to action and adventure as she was. Kowerski was a member of Poland's only motorized unit, the "Black Brigade." Granville felt he was the embodiment of the spirit of the Polish Resistance. Despite Granville being married, there was intense chemistry between her and Kowerski that would later result in an affair, which would be kept secret due to the nature of their occupations.

In late February of 1940, Christine Granville had still not been able to cross the border to Poland. The cause for this, according to the British, came from the Polish Resistance itself. The leading Resistance group was concerned that Granville would be a liability; she was an amateur and operating on the "side" of the British - those that seemed to have failed the Poles. She was sorely mistaken if she believed that putting her life on the line for her nation would mean acceptance. Once again, she felt alienated, only now her 'otherness' was not ascribed to her Jewish roots but rather to her being a British agent. Granville attempted to downplay the hostility in her report to Section D, but their support for her dwindled.

At the end of February, with the help of Kowerski, Granville would find her first opportunity to carry British propaganda into the area of occupied Poland. After Radzimiński's dismissal in Budapest (he had become obsessed with Granville and threatened to commit suicide if he could not be with her), Granville introduced Kowerski to the British Secret Service. She told her superiors at Section D that he was the only person she could trust. He, in turn, introduced her to Polish Olympic skier Janek Marusarz who was now working as a mountain courier for the Polish Military Attaché.

Much to Marusarz's initial amusement, Granville asked him to take her on his next journey into Slovakia. This journey included hiking over the High Tatra Mountains at an elevation of 2,000 meters, crossing the Polish border undetected, and skiing down into Zakopane. When Marusarz realized she was serious, he began to think she might be insane. Not only would they need to do this in the middle of the war, but that year's winter was also the worst in living memory, and there were no ski paths or roads. They would have to ski into Poland and then complete a hike of several days up the mountains on the other side of the border, all while carrying potentially incriminating supplies and illegal documents. Marusarz doubted that she would be able to survive that, and, at first, Kowerski supported him. However, both men underestimated Granville's charm and powers of persuasion, and soon they made the necessary arrangements for their journey.

One week later, Kowerski drove Marusarz, a man known only as Richard, and Granville to the Keleti station in Budapest, where they would take a train to the Polish border. Granville assumed the name 'Zofia Andrzejewska' for this mission in honor of her lover remaining behind in Budapest. They spent the night in a safe house and caught an early connecting train into Czechoslovakia. Before reaching the first station, they jumped out of the carriage with their heavy wooden skis and poles.

They began their two days of climbing. At first, Granville stumbled in Marusarz's tracks while switching between carrying or wearing her skis. She later stated that it was so cold that the breaths she took hurt her throat and lungs, and her fingers were frozen. They spent the first night huddled up in a little wooden hut to try and keep warm. By the end of the second afternoon, they had reached Cicha Dolina; this was the valley used by thieves and traders to reach Zakopane. That evening, a blizzard blew up, and they, once again, spent the night in a hut. Granville was sure she heard someone shouting at one point, but the blizzard was so extreme they could not see outside or dare to leave the hut. The blizzard had blown over by the following morning, and they left early to make the most of the day. Due to the clear weather, their view of the area around them improved, but they were also more vulnerable to being spotted by border patrols. But while the weather seemed almost lovely, Granville would encounter her first casualty of war before reaching Zakopane. Halfway up the ascent, the trio spotted two rucksacks in the snow, not containing any papers. A short distance away from the abandoned rucksacks, they found the bodies of a young lady and a young man, clearly attempting to cross into neutral territory, huddled together and holding hands. This unnecessary loss deeply shook Christine Granville. She covered their faces and drew a cross in the snow above their heads, the only burial she could give them. "Here are your Germans," Granville's last words before the three travelers finished their climb in silence (Mulley, 2014).

After the physical and emotional strain of the hike, the ski down into Zakopane provided Granville with some release. Marusarz's parents welcomed her warmly and with open arms once they arrived. After resting and regaining her strength, she sent a postcard to Kowerski to let him know she made it safely. Granville soon began her work. Zakopane was full of Wehrmacht officers, but she still secretly met with a number of her old friends and managed to secure their support. Granville also gained support from several highlanders who were already transporting people and goods over the mountains. And a few days later, she was on a train to Warsaw.

Unfortunately, Granville had some trouble on the train to Warsaw. She was carrying quite a few incriminating documents with her and was faced with the possibility of being discovered by one of the armed guards doing random checks. But ever the quick thinker, Granville managed to charm one of the Gestapo officers into believing she was smuggling black-market tea to her sick mother. She even managed to convince him to keep her parcel safe until they reached Warsaw central station. Upon arrival, she saw that this was not the Warsaw she remembered. The station was left untouched by the Nazi bombings, but the buildings in the capital were not offered the same mercy. Granville was supposed to blend in once she reached Warsaw and draw as little suspicion as possible to herself. She was, however, too shocked by the state of things to keep up pretenses. Instead, she walked to her mother's apartment; Stefania still lived in the same house she once shared with her two children. Granville spent two days with her mother, who had refused to register as a Jew, before slipping away into the city. She feared that staying any longer would further endanger her mother's life.

And so, her struggles with the underground Polish Resistance began. The Resistance, also referred to as the 'Home Army,' would grow significantly during the war, but when Granville first arrived in 1940, the Resistance was still very split and unorganized. She asked trusted friends to introduce her to members of various Resistance groups, but she was not discreet enough. Granville had told the tale of their trek across the mountain to multiple people, making her easy to identify, and soon Resistance networks were unsure whether they could trust her. One of these networks, the ZWZ, regarded her as a British agent that needed to be treated with extreme caution. The group had deemed her a liability, not only because she was working with British intelligence but also because she was well-known in the Polish capital and far too inexperienced for covert operations. However, Granville was undeterred by the ZWZ's doubt and, instead, continued to attempt to work with other Resistance groups. This was how she made contact with the Musketeers and their leader Stefan Witkowski. He would introduce her to several people, including Michal Gradowski; Gradwoski was a courier on the Warsaw-Budapest route and would soon begin enlisting Granville to carry microfilm into Hungary.

She spent some time in Warsaw, but after being recognized, she chose to remain outside of the capital and gather intel from other Resistance groups and observe what was happening in the surrounding areas. Granville returned to Warsaw two weeks after her first meeting with Witkowski and retrieved a small package of microfilm she needed to smuggle back to Hungary. He had arranged for her to join a ZWZ courier who was also headed to Budapest. The courier was Count Władimir Ledóchowski. The two would become quick friends and even quicker lovers. Granville, Ledóchowski, and their guide caught a train heading for the mountains one afternoon. After several hours of strenuous hiking, they finally passed the concrete posts marking the border of Slovakia; and there their love affair began. It took several days for them to reach the Hungarian border. As they grew closer, Granville became more morose. She was now away from the action she craved so dearly and said to Ledóchowski "I feel my holiday is over" (Mulley, 2014). It was only when they reached Budapest, and he informed her he had no place to stay, that she brightened up again.

Danger In Hungary and Danger On The Road

Back in Budapest, Granville, Ledóchowski, and her left-behind lover Kowerski began working together. There was some animosity between the gentlemen, but both knew where they stood with Granville. Even though they carried some resentment toward the other male, they stood by their sense of duty to their country. Granville's husband Gizycki had been pressing for news of his wife. Still, between her delicate work and the tensions rising in Europe, it was difficult for her to communicate with him, let alone return to London to see him. So instead, she continued with her work.

She handed over the microfilm she carried for the Musketeers to Section D's Harrison as soon as she got to Budapest. She was now the group's reception point for couriers bringing information from Poland and soon became a secondary courier across the Tatra mountains. To Granville and Kowerski, the British had failed to do anything of substance with the intelligence provided, so they began to work more broadly with other Allied representatives in Budapest. Granville was recalled to London at one point, but due to Harrison being away and German forces spreading through Europe, she was temporarily cut off from her income and London. She applied to be a part of Polish intelligence in Budapest, but they still distrusted her. When explaining the decision, one officer stated, "We are the Polish Underground, and we do not wish the British to peek inside our underpants" (Mulley, 2014). They were still worried that Granville would relay their secrets and plans to the British, resulting in the British interfering in the work of the Resistance movements.

In the meantime, they learned that when the sudden German invasion happened, state-of-the-art, high-velocity Polish rifles were never used, and their blueprints were quickly destroyed. The only way to recreate these in the future would be to apply reverse engineering to an existing rifle. Kowerski had used such a rifle while he was still in Poland and, when he began his plan to cross over into Budapest, had hidden it by burying it in a sealed box in the forest on his family's old estate. So, he contacted a distant cousin in the Polish Resistance and asked him to retrieve the rifle for Kowerski, who would hand it over to people who would be able to work with it.

Kowerski's cousin, Ludwig, agreed to help him with this dangerous task. Accompanied by a friend, he used the same terrifying path to cross the mountain into Poland as Granville had done. He traveled to Kowerski's family estate and retrieved the rifle. The two men managed to smuggle the gun into Budapest a few days later; they had sawn off the stock and barrel in order to bring the rifle into Budapest undetected. Foolishly, the two men decided that the best place to hide the gun would be under Ludwig's bed.

Ludwig and his friend met with Granville and Kowerski at a bar after they had hidden the rifle. They had not been together for long before the group broke into a long and heated argument over what needed to be done with the rifle. Granville soon grew irritated with the men and their arguments and decided to leave the fate of the gun up to them. When Ludwig returned home later that evening, he was shocked to see that the Hungarian Police had ransacked his apartment, now filled with pro-Nazi officers. As if that was not bad enough, he was terrified when he discovered that the rifle was missing. Ludwig was ready to flee because he thought he had been compromised, when Granville knocked on his door. She listened, presumably very amused, to Ludwig as he attempted to explain the predicament they were in. Once he was finished, Granville revealed that none of them were compromised or in danger. She had gone to his apartment earlier that afternoon, broken into his room, and taken the rifle. After dismantling the gun, she had sewn it into her mattress back in her apartment in Derék Utca. Granville had beaten the police by about an hour. She told Ludwig that she would be delivering the gun to the French herself.

With no income and no apparent support, Granville continued to act as a courier for messages and information between those in Warsaw and those in Budapest. Unfortunately, she would soon not be able to do that either. On one such mission to attempt to cross into Warsaw, she discovered an increase in border guards and floods that would make it impossible to cross into Poland. Granville was frustrated and would remain that way until another mission crossed her path. Then, finally, luck would be on her side; Ledóchowski would receive an assignment that Granville could accompany him on. He had been tasked with smuggling microfilm of papers confirming the promotion of a commander to the rank of General.

Kowerski had driven them to the train station, and the next day Ledóchowski and Granville took a taxi towards the mountains. They began hiking on the most hidden paths they could find until they entered the forests near the border. It was nearing midnight before the pair decided to stop and sleep. However, at dawn the following morning, they realized they had walked in a circle and were close to the Hungarian border, near a Slovak checkpoint. At this point, the Hungarian police were more or less controlled by the Gestapo, and travelers had to be extremely careful. They narrowly avoided being caught once but would not be so successful a second time. Finally, they had reached a railway station, hoping to begin the final leg of their journey to Warsaw, when they came face-to-face with an armed guard. Ledóchowski tried to explain that he and his sister, Granville, had escaped from an internment camp in Budapest and were simply heading home to Poland. While the guard seemed sympathetic, an armed patrol still arrived to escort them to the nearest police station and, the next day, to be questioned by the Gestapo.

Unfortunately, Granville and Ledóchowski made some questionable decisions while attempting to keep their cover. As a result, they and their bags were searched. Ledóchowski's Madonna medal would give him away; this had come to be regarded as a ZWZ tag. He realized he was now a liability. "Feeling he was ready to die" (Mulley, 2014), he began to consider how to go about it but was loath to do anything rash. By 2 a.m, the Gestapo had still not arrived, and the pair began to contemplate escape. Ledóchowski concluded that if they could cause enough distraction, they would be able to disappear into the forest some 50 meters behind them. Thankfully, Granville began to fight with a guard over a necklace Ledóchowski had gifted her. In the confusion created by the fight, he was able to grab her and drag her to the embankment. Granville had injured her leg, but both left the encounter relatively unscathed. After one final close encounter with a patrol who shot at them, they reached a space near the top of the mountains where they could rest. Two days later, they crossed the Hungarian border, and the following evening, they were reunited with Kowerski. Unfortunately, their mission was unsuccessful, Ledóchowski's Polish commanders were furious that he had been compromised. He was ordered to either rejoin the Polish Army in Poland or in the Middle East. A few days later, Ledóchowski moved to Belgrade.

Despite the work they were doing in Budapest, Granville and Kowerski were not safe. Conditions in Budapest grew more and more dangerous by the day, and neither of them had diplomatic immunity. Granville had managed to gain the trust and help of the British Minister in Hungary, Sir Owen O'Malley. But their allyship and eventual friendship with him could not protect them. By January 1941, it came to Kowerski's attention that he and Granville were being monitored constantly. He had practiced various escape routes, but all for naught; in late January 1941, either the 24th or 25th, they were accosted in Christine Granville's apartment and arrested for questioning. Neither would be able to withstand invasive questioning for very long, especially not Granville, who was already sick. Ever the thinker and planner, she used her illness to their advantage. She increased her coughing and made it seem harsher than it actually was. To convince the Germans of her sickness even further, she bit her own tongue; this ensured that she would also cough up blood. The Germans were incredibly scared of tuberculosis and contacted a prison doctor to examine Granville. The doctor had taken Granville to get her chest X-rayed, and, lo and behold, she had dark spots on her lungs (a result of the fumes from her previous job at the Fiat dealership). Both Granville and Kowerski were released, as the Gestapo believed both to be contagious. However, there were certain conditions to their release and soon after, they realized not only were their phones bugged but they were still being followed.

O'Malley began making arrangements for them to leave Hungary. He supplied them with false passports; they officially became Anthony Kennedy and Christine Granville. With these new documents, she also changed her year of birth to 1915, which would cause historians great confusion. Granville would be smuggled out of Hungary in the trunk of a Chrysler, with Kowerski following in an Opel closely behind. The couple were reunited in Yugoslavia. Kowerski later stated that the whole situation was one big adventure to Granville, "like it was a picnic" (Mulley, 2014).

They arrived in Belgrade soon after and introduced themselves to the British Legation. The pair had some time to relax, and, despite Granville's persistent cough, they felt safe. They were later joined by O'Malley, who boasted to the British about Granville and her courage. Of course, there was no need for that; the British intelligence was eager to keep Granville and Kowerski employed. In 1940, Section D had closed down, and Winston Churchill launched the SOE. During her days of carrying evidence across borders, Granville would carry the first film evidence of Nazi preparation for the invasion of an Allied country, the Soviet Union. Churchill's daughter, Sarah Oliver, had said that when the films were given to her father, he remarked that Granville was indeed his favorite spy.

At this point, all SOE operations in the Balkans and the Middle East were conducted from Cairo, though in later years, more stations would open. Granville would become familiar with all of them, but in Belgrade her old Section D contact George Taylor met her as head of the SOE's Balkan section. Taylor had to find someone to replace Granville as their contact in Budapest. Much to Kowerski's dismay, she suggested her husband Gizycki; his practical skills and fluency in multiple languages made him an excellent choice. With Taylor's approval, she wrote to her husband and asked to meet him in Istanbul, where she would convince him to take her position in Budapest.

Kowerski and Granville set out in the Opel, with Egypt as their end destination in mind. However, their first stop would be in Sofia,

Bulgaria, where they reported to the British Legation on the last Sunday in February 1941. There they met Aidan Crawley, who received microfilm from Granville with information that could potentially change the course of the war. The microfilm contained photos of weapons, ammunition, and hundreds of tanks gathered at Russia's eastern border. This intel would be sent to Churchill and change how the British approached their campaign. Once thoroughly debriefed, Granville would file her report, and Kowerski officially became an SOE officer.

Their next stop was Istanbul, Turkey. Despite Turkey remaining neutral during the war, the pair were still stopped at the border. To their frustration and the guards' amusement, they had to unpack every single thing in the car and wait until dawn before they could cross the border. When they finally arrived in Istanbul, they were struck by the strange sense of quiet, after the chaos of Europe. The only information available from Granville's SOE records states that "in Istanbul, she assisted our Polish Section in their courier and contact work" (Mulley, 2014). She ensured that the courier routes used by Resistance members remained functional and sent the correct information and funds to the Musketeers. Gizycki arrived in Istanbul on the 17th of March 1941, and immediately received Granville's address from the SOE. While there seemed to be no animosity between the couple, even though he knew about her affair with Kowerski, the latter seemed quite fearful of Granville's husband. Nevertheless, Gizycki agreed to take over Granville's former job and the next few days were spent debriefing him.

Not long after her husband left for Budapest, the couple were on the road again. This time they were determined to reach their final destination - Cairo. Granville somehow managed to procure some travel visas to move through pro-Vichy Syria and Lebanon. In mid-May, they crossed the border into Syria. From there, they traveled to Palestine, where they checked in with the British authorities. Granville and Kowerski played tourist for a while, almost able to forget about the war raging in Europe. Then, not even two weeks later, they were summoned to Cairo. The Opel eventually crossed the final border into Egypt. While the couple thought that reaching Cairo might solve some of their issues, they would soon learn this was anything but true. Instead, they were questioned separately about their loyalty to the Polish cause.

Aristocrat In Shining Armor

Despite her somewhat rocky relationship with the SOE, Granville would continue to work for them until the end of the war. One of her most heroic feats would occur in 1944, as Allied forces made their way through Europe, freeing occupied countries from German troops. Francis Cammaerts, leader of the Jockey network in France, needed a new courier after his previous female courier was captured and killed. Granville, desperate to be dropped into France, would be a great successor. Her mission was launched from Algiers, a base of the AMF section - one of several branches in France. As Jaqueline Armand, codenamed 'Pauline,' she parachuted into France in July 1944. Granville was armed and issued a rubber-lined helmet, a cyanide tablet, and some French papers forged by Polish and British professionals. Despite the terrible weather they faced when having to be dropped, Granville was not scared; if anything, she was excited and exhilarated.

Granville was now officially part of the Jockey network. She met Cammaerts a few days later, who would later mention that "even in those rough conditions [he] was impressed by her features and bearing" (Mulley, 2014). They got along immediately; he had a good sense of right and wrong and was incredibly meticulous and dedicated. Granville had been sent to France with two main objectives: she would primarily act as a courier for Cammaerts and local Resistance leaders and help subvert Polish and other foreign units fighting for the German army. Both Granville and Cammaerts believed that their chief aim should be to persuade as many people as possible to join their cause. Sylviane Rey, a friend of Granville's during this time, would remember that during their first meeting, "she created a climate of warm friendship so rapidly that one felt one had known her forever" (Mulley, 2014). The close friendship between Cammaerts and Granville would later develop into a passionate love affair while both were still active agents in the field. After the war ended, the pair would remain very close friends; he would recommend her for jobs, always carried her best interest at heart, and even named his daughter after Christine.

While in France, Granville did an incredible amount of work for the Jockey network. The network generally praised her for her dedication to her tasks. But there is one mission she undertook that would be far more dangerous and associated with her name for years to come. In

August 1944, Cammaerts, Xan Fielding (another SOE agent), and Christian Sorensen (a French officer) were arrested at a roadblock by the Gestapo. Despite their best attempts to pretend they were strangers to one another, the banknotes in their wallets (all from the same series) gave them away. The men were taken to Digne prison; the circumstances were similar to the first prison Virginia Hall's fellow agents found themselves in. After 24 hours, they were taken to the Villa Marie-Louise, located on the outskirts of Digne. The Villa was a well-known Gestapo headquarters and a place where Resistance members were taken to be tortured.

Those questioning them had very little information about who they actually were and who they were working for, yet the three men were condemned to be executed. The men knew that the Allies should have landed near Digne by this time and that the area would soon be liberated, but it might still be too late to save them. Granville had arrived back at their base to hear that the men had been condemned to execution. She spent a few days trying to convince some of the local Resistance groups to help her free the captured men. Unfortunately, the Resistance leaders decided that the risk was simply too significant.

Granville might have been distraught, but she was never distracted from her true job. She had sent messages to the new agents parachuting into France in Cammaerts' absence and ordered them to help with subverting the remaining foreign troops still on the Germans' side. When Granville learned the date of their execution, the 17th of August, she now had to decide if taking the risk could be justified. In the end, it was determined that Cammaerts was too important to the Jockey network not to attempt to rescue him and the other two men.

With her mind made up, Granville traveled to Digne on a bicycle. Once there, she entered the grounds alongside family members, searching for some news about their imprisoned relatives. Granville walked along the courtyard and hummed the tune of 'Frankie and Johnny;' a song she and Cammaerts sang whenever they needed to keep their spirits lifted. Cammaerts responded in turn but thought she was there to say goodbye. However, to Granville, this was the confirmation she needed that the men were indeed there, and she proceeded to approach Albert Schenck. Schenck was somewhat of a double agent, at least in his mind. To justify her concern for

Cammaerts without revealing his importance, she pretended to be his wife. She thought her best option would be to scare him into helping her. Granville informed him that an Allied attack was imminent and that he would be handed over to the mobs once they had seized the prison. Schenck told her the only person that could help her was Max Waem, and for a ransom of two million French francs, he could bribe Waem into meeting with her.

Christine Granville cycled back to her base after the meeting, determined to free her colleagues. She had managed to arrange for the ransom to be delivered in 48 hours; this would be one of the quickest responses to a request she had ever had. Two days later, she cycled back to Digne and proceeded to, once again, frighten and threaten Schenk with the Allied forces. Only after he was sufficiently frightened did she hand over the money. He arranged for her to meet with Waem that afternoon. Granville reported that "when he came, he at first covered [her] with his revolver" (Mulley, 2014). The revolver was soon lowered, and after a conversation lasting three hours, Warm agreed to help free the three men. He had three conditions, however. After the war, he wanted to be treated as a free man, he wanted to be able to return to France and convince the people of his complete innocence, and he wanted to partake in some missions for the British. Their contract's exact terms and conditions are uncertain, but Granville managed to secure his help two hours before the men were due to be executed.

That evening, after a surprisingly fine dinner, the three men were marched across the prison courtyard by Waem. Outside of the gates, they expected to be guided to the fields used by the firing squad for executions, but they were steered the other way. They soon reached a car where Waem ordered them to get in, after which he proceeded to get in beside the driver himself. As Waem was wearing his uniform jacket, the sentries did not hesitate to let them pass through the gate and drive away from the prison. Around the first bend from the prison, they stopped to pick up a lonely figure; Christine Granville. Cammaerts feared that she had been captured as well. It was only after they were further away from the prison and helping Waem dispose of his uniform jacket that Cammaerts realized Granville had rescued them. Instead of a senseless execution, their night would be filled with celebrations. All thanks to Christine Granville.

After The War

Life after the war was not kind to Christine Granville. Not only was her life of constant adventure coming to an end, but new challenges would await her no matter the direction she wished to take with her new life. It was clear that Granville would struggle to transition from the constant drama of life in the war years to the quiet routines of peace. Her post-war story would be dominated by men, politics, depression, and a longing for adventure she never quite managed to satiate.

The SOE, which Granville had become an agent of after it was established, was disbanded soon after the war. Both Granville and Kowerski were left without an income, although Kowerski settled in Germany and went into business, much to Granville's disapproval. Not only was she quickly left without any financial resources, but Granville also struggled to find a country that would provide her with citizenship. Any Poles outside of Poland were not allowed back into the country at that stage and were also not considered citizens. And if Granville thought that her service and accomplishments during the war would make becoming a British citizen easy, she would be mistaken. Due to the constant change of identity and forged papers during the war, she was denied citizenship several times, and the process was difficult and drawn out each time, despite reaching out to her male friends, allies, and former colleagues. However, she did finally receive a passport stating she had been granted the status of British citizenship by naturalization.

Not all was bad during this time. Granville was honored for her actions during the war, although not in the same ways as her male counterparts despite, in some cases, being more daring and delivering better results than they did. For saving her comrades from certain execution in Digne, she was awarded the George Medal. In May 1947, Granville was appointed an OBE for her work alongside the British empire. This was not usually given to military personnel with a lower rank than lieutenant colonel and certainly above an MBE, usually awarded to other female agents who worked with the SOE. Granville was also honored with the Croix de Guerre for aiding France in her time of need and for contributing to the country's liberation. France also awarded her the Order of Vercors, "a combatant's medal... which she claimed to value even more" (Mulley, 2014). Finally, despite her rocky relationship with the Polish authorities and the Resistance during the war, she was treated with the utmost respect when she visited the Polish military headquarters in 1945.

But these honors, her courage during the war, and her dedication to the cause, meant little once the SOE disbanded and she could find no one willing to help her. Granville kept in regular contact with Kowerski; there would always be a bond between them, and they would always care for each other on a deeper level. In the meantime, she tried her hand at various jobs to make ends meet. From telephone operator to salesperson to waitress – gone was the glamor and danger that she had experienced as a special agent. Her lust for adventure had not abated and she struggled to find a place in post-war society. After she and Kowerski lost most of their money in an investment in Australia gone awry, in 1951, Granville took a job as a stewardess aboard a passenger ship called *Ruahine*. It is believed she thought the constant travel might inject some adventure back into her life.

However, life was not easy on board the ship either. The captain had ordered the crew to wear any wartime decorations they might have, which drew some unwanted attention to Granville. She soon became the focus of xenophobic and disparaging discussions among her crewmates, who viewed her with hostility and resentment. One crew member, Dennis Muldowney, took Granville's side and defended her against the slew of abuse she faced. There is some dispute about whether or not their newfound friendship led to a physical relationship. Still, it was certain that throughout this entire time, Granville remained emotionally faithful to Kowerski.

By 1952, Granville had grown bored and tired of life at sea and was even more frustrated with Muldowney's obsession with her. He mistook her gratefulness for genuine romantic love and adoration and would not leave her alone. She had dismissed him and told him she would be joining Kowerski in Germany. At the time, some believed Granville and Kowerski would finally be married. Unfortunately, Muldowney firmly believed that if he could not have Christine Granville, no one could. On the 15th of July 1952, Muldowney cornered her in a hotel and stabbed her in the chest; she was dead within seconds. When confessing, Muldowney would say, "to kill is the final possession" (Mulley, 2014). Kowerski would be the one to identify her body, and a week later, Christine Granville would be buried at Kensal Green in London. It might not have been the heroic death she had once wished for, but Christine Granville certainly left the world surrounded by danger and action, things she could not live without.

As strange as it might sound, despite all the horrors and violence, Granville, just like Virginia Hall, felt liberated by the war and the chances it afforded her to prove herself, free from the limitations of her previous role as a high-society lady. There is no doubt that her achievements during the war were extraordinary. She was the first woman to serve in the field as a special agent for the British, she was the longest-serving female agent for the British, and she delivered some of the most crucial intelligence ever to reach Britain during the war. So much of what Granville achieved could not have been done if she were a man. How tragic that she was denied the chance to discover herself after the war; she never had the opportunity to find out who or what she could have been in a world freed from war.

What saddens many about the life of Christine Granville is that her tales and heroics were constantly overshadowed by the men she was surrounded with. She was a woman who enjoyed spending time with men; that much is true. But none of the stories of her dangerous missions are told without mentioning men who fell in love with her or whom she had a relationship with. Granville was an exceptional woman who did extraordinary things, but the focus of interest has always been on her sexual and romantic liaisons, rather than on her contributions to the Allied war effort. Even in death, Granville could not escape the shadow of the men in her life. But her killer, Muldowney, was mistaken about possessing Christine by extinguishing her life. No one ever had or could ever possess Christine Granville. Only her own passion for liberty could possibly possess her. Christine Granville could be cruel and ruthless, but she loved fiercely and was incredibly dedicated to every cause she believed in and every task she undertook.

Chapter 5:

The Antipodean Rebel – Nancy Wake

AUSTRALIAN WAR MEMORIAL   P00885.001

Figure 3: Nancy Wake, 1945, Australian War Memorial.

Growing up far from where she would later throw herself into danger for others, Nancy Wake was familiar with living both in poverty and, later, lavishly. There was never a moment where she believed that women needed to stay behind and watch men trot off to war. She thought that women could be just as strong, valiant, and ruthless as men. Like Hall and Granville, Wake did not hesitate to jump headfirst into the Second World War, leaving her rich society life behind.

Born Far From Future War

Not much information is available about Nancy Wake's life before she was inexorably drawn towards the French Resistance during the Second World War. The few available details reveal a glimpse into how a single gift offered her a way out of a life of poverty and led her to one of glamour, riches and, later, adventures. Born on the 30th of August 1912, in Wellington, New Zealand, Wake was the youngest of six children. In 1914, before the age of two, Wake's parents decided to move their family to Australia, where she would live until she was 16 years old. Her childhood was filled with instability and poverty, worsened by her father's leaving. Shortly after moving to Australia, her father returned to New Zealand under the pretense of filming a documentary on the Maori tribe. It would have seemed perfectly acceptable, as Wake was descended from the Maori through her great-grandmother. However, the reality was that her father abandoned his family and left her mother to raise six children.

Wake attended the North Sydney Household Arts School in Sydney, Australia. However, the life she lived while there had no appeal to her. At the age of 16, she ran away from her family and began working as a nurse in other parts of Australia. Her life would change forever when Wake received a gift, sometimes described as an inheritance, of $200 from her aunt. In modern times, $200 might not seem like much, but at that time it was a large amount of money.

So, Wake decided to take the money and leave Australia. She traveled to New York and then headed to England. While in England, Wake took a course in journalism that landed her a job at the Chicago Tribune, and this job would take her to Paris. With a stable income in France, she began to enjoy an extravagant life and felt settled in France. She met her future husband, wealthy industrialist Henri Fiocca, in 1937, and in November 1939, the two got married. With her income and her husband's wealth, Wake could fully enjoy the Parisian social life. Nancy Wake quickly went from being a poor young nurse in Australia to a wealthy socialite in France, but her newfound wealth would not define her. During the war, Wake's contribution would prove that you should never judge a book by its cover.

From The High Life To The Front Lines

As a journalist in Europe during the 1930s, Wake had a front-row seat to the rise of Hitler and his followers. During a trip to Vienna, Austria, she witnessed Nazi gangs abusing and beating Jewish men and women in the streets. What she saw with her own eyes in some European countries and the anti-Semitism she heard appalled her. When asked about it later, Wake recalled being horrified by what she saw and immediately deciding to do something about it. Before Hitler gained power and the Nazis officially began to take control of Europe, Wake had already vowed to get involved in any way she could. Her husband shared her feelings on the matter, and the couple would, at the beginning of the war, work together to help as many people as they could.

Wake and Fiocca lived in Marseille in the south of France when the German troops invaded the country. The couple's wealth and high status in society afforded them some safety during the initial invasions. Wake was living a double life as a secret agent and a wife, a life she relished. As the war progressed, both Wake and her husband became involved in the fledgling Resistance. They helped the Resistance by couriering small packages and assisting those escaping from France across the Pyrenees. The Resistance started as a way of fighting against the German troops who took over France, and Wake, who would not pass up an opportunity to work against the Nazis, was incredibly eager to join them and help. They were quick to decide that they would use their wealth to help allied soldiers and Jews escape from France whenever they could. Some reports state that Wake bought an ambulance to help her transport refugees to Spain's safe and neutral territory. Along with assisting refugees to escape into secure areas, Wake transported equipment needed by the local Resistance.

Wake soon appeared on the Gestapo's radar and was the cause of immense frustration. No matter what approach they took, she continuously evaded them. Wake had been known to use her attractiveness as a tool to get what she wanted. She would outsmart guards at enemy checkpoints, flirt with them to distract them, be let through, and use numerous false identities. Being part of the Resistance network and her constant evasion of detection led to Wake becoming the Gestapo's most wanted Resistance member, with a large bounty on her head for her capture. They nicknamed her the White Mouse - a pest the Gestapo could not catch or get rid of.

Due to the Gestapo's interest in her, Marseilles was soon too dangerous for Wake to live and operate in. The only way she could continue aiding the Resistance would be to flee France. In 1943, Fiocca and Wake decided that she must leave the country and go to England until she was able to safely return. It took six attempts for Wake to escape from France and cross the Pyrenees into Spain. One attempt resulted in her arrest by the French police. She was questioned for some time but persuaded them to let her go. When she finally reached Spain, Wake took a ship to England and headed to London. Fiocca stayed in Marseilles and aided the Resistance but was soon captured by the Gestapo and questioned about his wife. He refused to provide any information about Wake and suffered the consequences for this loyalty; he was brutally tortured by the Gestapo and eventually killed. While in Spain and England, Wake refused to contact her husband for fear of putting him in more danger. Nancy Wake would not learn of his death until near the end of the war; the torment of guilt and grief she then felt fueled her fight against the Nazis.

Becoming A (Still Wanted) Spy

Once Wake reached Britain, she was quickly recruited to join the SOE. With its inception, the SOE believed that Nazi ideology was steeped in misogyny, so they would be less likely to suspect a woman of being a spy. For this reason, it was easier for women (at this time) to join the SOE and help in the field during the war. Wake was one of 39 women that would become part of this intelligence organization during World War II.

Wake spent some months training with the SOE and developing various skills that would aid her in the field. Some reports of her time in training indicate that Wake had no trouble during training and excelled in everything she did. She began working in the French section of the SOE and, from the very start, wanted to return to France as quickly as she possibly could. Wake's specialist training included handling a variety of weapons, silent killing, survival skills, sabotage, hand-to-hand combat, and explosives. By April 1944, Wake was ready to return to France and begin her first assignment.

In April 1944, Wake was part of a three-person team that parachuted into Auvergne, France. Her other team members included John Hind Farmer, the head of the group, and Denis Rake, the radio operator. Rake and Wake would become close friends during the time they worked together. Interestingly, Rake had also served as Virginia Hall's radio operator. Wake had several duties during her time in Auvergne. She had to organize and pinpoint locations where resources would be parachuted in, collect them, and allocate them to the local Resistance groups. Along with her fellow agents and Resistance members, she would help organize the Resistance and weaken the German forces in the area to prepare for the Allied invasion. Nancy Wake would be known as one of the most capable Resistance fighters, despite the first Maquis leader she met planning to kill her ('Maquis' was the name used for groups of paramilitary Resistance fighters in France), and she would lead thousands of fighters in guerilla attacks against German troops.

Chapter 6:

The White Mouse –
A Perfect Fighter

Nancy Wake was one of the most honored and decorated women who aided the Resistance during the Second World War. She did some truly incredible things with the Resistance groups in occupied France; some of which stood out more than others.

Games Of Cat And Mouse

Arrested While Fleeing

Before Wake became an operative for the SOE, she had already been extremely high on the Gestapo's radar. They were actively looking for her as she was helping refugees flee to neutral territories around France. As mentioned earlier, this resulted in Wake needing to flee from her home in Marseilles and leave France. It took several attempts for her to safely cross the Pyrenees and reach the neutral territory of Spain.

One of these attempts to escape the clutches of the Nazis resulted in her arrest. While hiding and waiting in Toulouse, Wake was arrested in a random round-up that included a large number of people. Fortunately, the French police that arrested her had no idea that they had one of the Gestapo's most wanted in their custody. Allegedly, Wake was being accused of being involved in blowing up a cinema; the accusation was entirely false, and it is possible that French police were using this as a way to flush out anyone who worked with the Resistance.

Wake spent four days being interrogated and beaten before someone she worked with in the Pat O'Leary network came to help her. Their group leader, Albert Guerisse, who had taken over from Ian Garrow, was the network member who came to Wake's aid. He convinced the authorities that the story Wake had given them was all a ruse. According to Guerisse, she was his mistress and that the story she had told them was a cover she used to deceive and escape from her husband. This was, of course, untrue as well. Besides working together aiding the Resistance, Guerisse and Wake had no relationship whatsoever. However, the police chief seemed to understand her dilemma and, out of some sense of sympathy, let her go. After four terrible days, Wake was free to continue making her way to Spain.

A Terrible Bike Ride

Soon after she parachuted into France to act as the liaison between London and the Maquis, Wake and her companions spent some time cut off from the SOE in London and could not receive any incoming resources. Though her initial relationship with the local Maquis in Auvergne was rocky, everyone was soon working together to prepare for D-Day (the day of the Allied forces' invasion of Normandy, France, which would free occupied forces from German control). But while Wake was fearless and bold in her attempts to weaken the Nazi posts around the area, the Gestapo was actively hunting for the woman making their lives difficult.

Some historians speculate that the Gestapo paid some members of the Maquis for inside information to find Wake; this is not confirmed, however, and all that is known for certain is that they managed to find the base camp Wake and the Resistance members used. The Gestapo then bombed and attacked their camp in the mountains, killing some of the group's members and destroying their radio and codes. Some versions told of this attack suggest that Denis Rake was the one to destroy his radio to avoid the Nazis obtaining their codes; others state that the radio was destroyed by accident during the attack. Either way, the group was now without their primary form of communication.

Several of the men at the camp volunteered to go out and look for a wireless operator to inform the officials in London of their destroyed radio. Wake, however, believed that it would be better for her to go on this mission. As a woman, she would not be scrutinized as closely and would disguise herself to proceed unnoticed or unquestioned through checkpoints. The men agreed, and Wake set out on her high-risk operation.

There were no vehicles available to the Resistance, so the only mode of transportation Wake had available was a bicycle. She cycled to the nearest town with an SOE contact but could not use the radio or get in touch with the radio operator. Wake's only choice was to continue cycling 310 miles to Chateauroux, where she knew she would be able to find someone to help her radio to London and explain their predicament.

Traveling there and back, Wake passed several German checkpoints. She was disguised as a housewife and used the story that she was on her way to her hometown to visit a family member; this innocent and inconspicuous disguise allowed her to pass through the checkpoints with relative ease. She cycled over terrible mountain trails and through occupied territories to find a radio. Two versions of this story exist as told by historians. One of the lesser-explored versions is that Wake found a radio she could take back to their camp and hauled the heavy equipment back over the mountain. The more widely-accepted version is that she managed to find a radio operator who allowed her to use his radio to contact those in London. She requested a new radio and informed them of the group's location so the resources would be dropped at the correct place.

Once she succeeded in contacting the SOE in London, she had to face the long bicycle ride back to the Resistance group's hideout. It took Wake three days to complete the entire journey to Chateauroux and back to Auvergne. However, she safely made it through the checkpoints on her way back, and the SOE managed to supply the group with a new radio along with other resources needed for their sabotage activities. Despite the discomfort she faced during and after the cycling adventure, Wake is known to have declared this as the greatest thing she did during the war. Without her 72-hour travel, Wake and her men might not have been able to weaken the German posts as much as they did before D-Day.

Leading Lady Of The Maquis

When Wake returned to France after her SOE training, part of her duties was to organize the Resistance fighters in preparation for D-Day and to weaken the German troops the Allies would face during their attack. Wake and her two team members worked closely with the Maquis, who were based in the Auvergne region, in the mountains. Nancy Wake would end up as the pseudo leader of the Maquis. It took some time for her to gain their trust, but they were soon more than willing to fight alongside her.

Her first encounter with a leader of the Maquis was less than pleasant. The leader, a man named Gaspard, resented working with women and the British and despised Wake, who was both a woman and someone sent to France by the British. Some reports state that he conspired to kill her, but Wake found out about his plans and fled higher into the mountains. Her second interaction with a leader of the Maquis was significantly smoother, and would pave the way for Wake and the men to weaken the German forces. She worked with Fournier, a Frenchman, who was much more receptive to her and the SOE's ideas and objectives.

Despite the men being slightly more open to her plans, they were slow to trust her. But she continuously demonstrated her bravery; Wake fought alongside the men and was always willing to take the same risks the others took. She led a team of about 7,000 men and launched guerilla attacks against the German forces, attempting to damage their supply lines and minimize their access to resources such as ammunition. The fact that Wake was also not one to shy away from a drink and could hold her alcohol better than some men certainly counted in her favor as well. Though this cannot be definitively proven, it is believed that Wake successfully led a raid on the Gestapo headquarters based in Montlucon. In addition, during the lead-up to the Allied forces arriving in Europe, Wake and her men waged intensive sabotage missions against the German posts and troops.

Wake was undoubtedly a woman the Resistance troops around her could look up to, but she was anything but a sweet, high-society lady. Despite living comfortably and lavishly before the war, Wake was not afraid to leave her wealth behind and enter the harsh circumstances of the war effort. She was ruthless when it came to the cause she was fighting for. After the war, Wake talked about two instances where she had to step in and kill enemy soldiers. During one of the raids she and her troops took part in, the men had captured a female German spy. Her men could not find it in them to kill the spy, so Wake took matters into her own hands. She felt it was part of her duty to ensure that she and her men would remain unnoticed and safe. On another attack on German forces, she killed a German soldier with her bare hands; she used a hand-to-hand combat technique taught by the SOE to kill the man before he could sound the alarm.

After southern France was invaded and liberated by the American military, Wake and her men, along with other Resistance groups, moved down from the mountains and began rounding up stray members of the Gestapo and Nazi groups still in France. It took two months for Paris to be liberated from German forces, and, during these two months, Wake and her men would lead many attacks on the remaining occupying forces in southern France. It was at this time, as the war was drawing to a close that Wake learned her husband had been killed before she returned to France as part of the SOE. Despite her devastation at the loss, Nancy Wake continued to celebrate the end of an awful time in Europe's history and was praised by her troops for her bravery and leadership.

A Decorated Woman

It is believed that Nancy Wake is one of the most decorated women to have served during the Second World War. She received multiple honors, awards, and medals from numerous countries for her contribution to the Resistance and duties during the war. Some of these were awarded to her directly after the war, others were presented to her later in her life. It is reported that Wake sold her medals towards the end of her life to support herself financially, as she felt that they would be of no use to her after her passing.

Directly after the end of the war, in July 1945, Wake was awarded the George medal by the British. This was the first honor she received. Up until 2006, she received diverse awards and honors. The United Kingdom awarded her with multiple medals and awards; the 1939-45

Star, the France and Germany Star, the Defense Medal, and the British War Medal 1939-45. France presented her with the French Croix de Guerre with a Star and two Palms and the French Officer of the Legion of Honor; the latter is the highest merit awarded by the French. In 1970, she was made a Chevalier of the Legion of Honor and was promoted in 1988 to Officer of the Legion of Honor. The French also awarded her with the French Medaille de la Resistance for her courageous endeavors during the war.

Wake received the Medal of Freedom from the United States, and she was made a Companion of the Order of Australia in 2004 and, in 2006, was awarded the Badge in Gold from New Zealand. Shortly after the end of the Second World War, she was recommended for awards and honors in Australia but was turned down. The decision was later reversed, but Wake felt that it was too little too late; decorations awarded decades after the war showed insufficient appreciation of what she had done. The medals awarded to Nancy Wake during her lifetime are now on display in the Australian War Memorial.

Along with all these impressive medals, awards and honors, Nancy Wake was praised in creative ways. Many biographies and novels were written about her, and movies and television shows were created with female spy characters modeled after Wake. When the war began, she was seen as nothing more than the young wife of a rich industrialist, but by the end of the war, she was reframed as a dauntless, competent, and resourceful leader.

A Long Life After The War

After the war, Wake returned to England and continued her work for the British SOE. She worked for the British Air Ministry and Intelligence division. However, like Hall and Granville, Nancy Wake was not entirely satisfied with her more peaceful life after the war. She soon realized that she could never feel fulfilled in a job behind a desk. A few years after the war, she decided to move back to Australia.

In Australia, she found an interest in the world of politics. She stood as a Liberal candidate in both 1949 and 1951. Wake settled down in Sydney and ran two campaigns for the Sydney seats of Kingsford

Smith and Barton. Despite Wake having a decent percentage of support in her campaign, she was unsuccessful both times she ran in the Australian Federal Elections. During her second attempt in 1951, she got within one hundred votes of the man who ended up taking the seat. But she soon became unhappy and restless in Australia and moved back to England in late 1951.

Back in England, she spent five years working as an intelligence officer for the Air Ministry in Whitehall and met RAF officer John Forward. Wake and Forward got along well. They shared the same interests and could understand what the other had gone through during the war. In 1957, she and Forward got married. Soon after their wedding, Wake resigned from her job as an intelligence officer, and she and her husband moved to Australia in the 1960s.

In 1966, Wake was endorsed as a Liberal candidate during that year's election but was, unfortunately, once again unsuccessful. Wake and Forward lived in Sydney until 1985. During that year, they left Sydney to retire in Port Macquarie, where the couple would live until her husband's death. In that same year, Wake published her autobiography, *The White Mouse*. After 40 years of marriage, John Forward passed away in 1997. Wake remained in Australia for a few years after her husband's death but decided to move back to England in 2001 to enjoy the social life of a member of a services club. She became a resident at the Stafford Hotel in St James' Place, which had been a British and American forces club during the war. The manager at the time had also worked for the Resistance in Marseilles. She rarely needed to pay for anything. Any costs were covered by the owners, who were extremely fond of her, or by anonymous donors. Closer to the end of her life, Wake retired to the Star and Garter Home for ex-servicemen and women, located in Richmond.

On the 7th of August 2011, Nancy Wake passed away quite peacefully, less than a month before her 99th birthday. Wake never had any children, but was surrounded by love, whether old war friends or younger acquaintances who admired all she did during the war. Her final request was that her ashes be scattered in the area where she fought alongside her men during the war. Some accounts state that her ashes were to be scattered in Auvergne, others in Montlucon. What is evident in the post-war life of Wake, in common with many other women who worked in special intelligence during the war, is that she could not easily settle into the routines of peace time after her adrenaline-filled years as a spy. She was ever the restless, traveling figure; independent until the day she died. Until her death, and for decades after, Nancy Wake would be praised for her courage during the war, especially because she showed such loyalty to a country half a world away from her birthplace.

Chapter 7:

The Overlooked Indian Princess – Noor Inayat Khan

Figure 4: Noor Inayat Khan, 1942, ©Imperial War Museum (HU 074868)

Raised to value peace and explore her creative side, Noor Inayat Khan had no initial interest in the looming World War. However, she would soon decide to become more active in preventing and combating the war. Join the life of a spy who was criticized too often and who received not nearly enough praise for her role.

A Happy Childhood

Noor Inayat Khan was born on the 1st of January 1914, in Moscow, Russia. Khan was a perfect example of a child born from a diverse family. Her father, Inayat Khan, was descended from a royal, Tipu Sultan, and came from a family of Indian Muslims. He was a musician, a Sufi master, and a Sufism preacher who lived in Europe. Sufism is a mystic practice in Islam. Through practice and belief, Muslims become nearer to Allah. In Sufi thought, it is believed that closeness to God can be realized during this life. Khan's mother was a poet and an American from Albuquerque, New Mexico. Her mother was born Ora Ray Baker but changed her name to Pirani Ameena Begum when she married Inayat Khan. She met her husband in America during his travels through the United States. Due to her father's royal ancestry, Khan was considered an Indian princess or a Sufi Muslim Princess.

Shortly after the onset of the First World War, Khan's parents decided to relocate the family. The Tsar's officers had advised her father to leave, due to the growing unrest in Moscow with the Russian Revolution brewing. The family left Russia on a sled, having to pass several barricades and roadblocks. They moved to London, where they lived in Bloomsbury. Khan and her siblings attended school in Notting Hill (she was the oldest of four children). In 1920, the family moved to France and settled in Suresnes near Paris. The house the family lived in was allegedly a gift to her father from a benefactor of the Sufi movement. From an early age, Khan was described as a selfless and giving person. She was a quiet, shy, and sensitive child with a big imagination.

When she was 13 years old, in 1927, her father very suddenly passed away while on a pilgrimage in India. While growing up, Khan was greatly influenced by her father, and she internalized his beliefs; this was reflected in some of her earlier writing pieces. After his death, she took over some responsibility for her grieving mother. She helped take care of her younger siblings during the time her mother was overtaken by grief. Khan and her family lived in France until she was 26 years old.

Khan was a very educated and brilliant young woman. She studied child psychology at the Sorbonne and music at the Paris Conservatory. The main focus of her musical studies was composing pieces for the piano and the harp. As a young adult, she made a career for herself as a writer; she published her poetry and children's stories in both English and French. Khan soon became a regular contributor to children's magazines and French radio. In 1939, before the start of the Second World War, Khan's book, *Twenty Jataka Tales*, was published in London. This book was inspired by the Jataka tales of the Buddhist tradition. Some of the stories in the book were English translations of the reincarnation stories of Buddha. Khan favored writing short stories for children and even illustrated some children's books.

When World War II began and France was invaded, Khan and her family fled to Bordeaux and boarded a ship to escape to England by sea. The family reached Cornwall by June 1940. Because of their upbringing, Khan and her brother initially wanted to remain away from the conflict as much as possible. Eventually, both decided that they must stand up for freedom from the forces of occupation, without going against their upbringing and beliefs.

A Peace-Loving Sufi's Dilemma

Khan's parents, and their extended family, were a peaceful group of people. She and her siblings were Muslim by birth and had a Sufi upbringing, and her father encouraged them to view the world in a peaceful way. Khan greatly admired Gandhi, his mission for Indian independence, and his policy of nonviolence. These ideals were held by her father, whom Khan had idolized. She had internalized his beliefs even as a young adult.

She was disgusted and shocked by the Nazi ideology. Her father preached that there should be a oneness of religions, so even if you believed differently from another person, you should still respect them and their beliefs. The Nazis' disregard for the Jewish people and the disrespect the Jewish population faced was appalling to her. She had held noble ideals from a young age and was selfless and giving. Khan's conscience would not permit her to just stand by and passively watch these terrible developments.

She and her brother, Vilayat, wanted to contribute to the war effort in a non-violent way. Neither of them was willing to kill another person, but both felt they could not sit idly by and watch others be killed. To them, it was not enough to oppose fascism; they felt morally obligated to step into a more active role during Europe's time of crisis. Both Khan and her brother decided to temporarily join the British forces attempting to aid those affected by the Nazis. Because they refused to kill anyone, their options were limited. For Khan, this meant joining the WAAF and later the SOE. Her brother volunteered for mine-sweeping. Khan, as a passionate advocate for Indian independence, had no reason to support the British in a patriotic way. She hoped that by actively helping during the war, she could help form a bridge between Indians and the English. This hope, and the faith she was raised with, made the British question whether or not she had the right sensibility for helping during the war. Despite their doubts about her, and Khan's proud statement that she would stand against them after the war in favor of assisting India, she would become an SOE operative.

A Pacifist Heading To The Frontlines

When first considering joining the war effort, Khan thought about receiving training through the Red Cross. She could help wounded soldiers while still maintaining her nonviolent beliefs. But this would not be enough for her; she wanted to help in a more significant way. As Khan was examining the limited amount of choices she had for joining the war, she determined that there was, at that stage, only one possible way she could help the cause. Subsequently, she joined the Women's Auxiliary Air Force (WAAF) in November 1940. After joining the WAAF, Khan was sent to train as a wireless operator. In 1941, she was assigned to the bomber training school. So, before joining the SOE, Khan was trained in both wireless telegraphy and how to handle explosives. Khan would undoubtedly be a first for the SOE: she was the only Muslim special agent, the only agent with an Asian background, and the first female wireless operator to go behind enemy lines in France.

In 1943, she was recruited to join the F (French) Section of the SOE. During the early interview stages of recruitment, she proved to be a very controversial candidate because of her honesty in expressing her pro-Indian independence views. Even if this was initially a shock to other agents, Khan was still an ideal candidate for the SOE; she was perfectly bilingual in French and English (with no accent), was extremely skilled as a wireless operator, and showcased an incredible speed when working in Morse code. The SOE was in desperate need of all these qualities. To work for the SOE, she needed to receive specialist training to work as a wireless operator in occupied France. Khan traveled to Wanborough Manor near Guildford in Surrey. From there, she was sent to Aylesbury in Buckinghamshire. Khan would be the first woman to enter the occupied territory in this role. Her prior training in wireless telegraphy gave her a head start on those who were training with her and who had just begun their training.

During the final stages of their training, the agents were transferred from Aylesbury to Beaulieu. Their security training would end with a practice mission and a mock interrogation. As a radio operator, Khan's practice mission would work as follows: she would have to work as if in a strange city and find a safe place to send a transmission to her instructors while being pursued by an unknown agent, all while attempting to remain undetected. The aim of the mission was to show trainee agents the circumstances under which they would have to work and ensure they would be able to complete the assigned missions.

Along with the practice mission, potential agents had to face a mock interrogation, similar to those conducted by the Gestapo. Even when captured, interrogated, and almost certainly tortured, the agents needed to be able to maintain their cover story. This final and ultimate exercise would contribute to the final decision of whether or not the agent was ready to enter the field and could be trusted not to put their fellow agents in jeopardy.

However, Khan only received a truly adequate report in one training field; as a radio operator. She had some difficulties, due to swollen fingers caused by chilblains, but quickly adapted and improved her speed at transmitting messages every day. In the other training fields, Khan was reported to be unsuitable for the field. She was afraid of weapons (though she attempted to get over that), she was too emotional and opinionated, she gave too much information when asked questions, and while she was a good runner, she was not physically suited for the strain the frontlines would have on one's body. A note in her finishing report also said that she would not be able to blend into a crowd adequately enough to hide.

Her final report, which was found in her file some time after the war, mentioned the following: "Not overburdened with brains but has worked hard and shown keenness, apart from some dislike of the security side of the course. She has an unstable and temperamental personality, and it is very doubtful whether she is really suited to work in the field" (Wikipedia Contributors, 2019a). It seemed like the universe was acting against Khan. She could not fully complete her security training because the SOE was desperate to send trained wireless telegraphy operators into France. It was also said that her gentle personality and childlike manner worried her instructors, and they believed she would not fare well in the field. One of the instructors' main concerns was that it seemed that Khan had come to the training and almost completed it without truly knowing what she would be getting into. In her biography, written by Shrabani Basu (2008), Colonel Frank Spooner later said that "he had prepared the harsh report just to protect Noor and to prevent her going into the field." Leo Marks, an agent at the training facilities, was asked to give her an extended briefing in which he learned that "she would rather die than tell a lie" (Basu, 2008). Regardless of this, her commitment to the cause could not be questioned. In the end, it was decided that Khan could enter the field and could successfully help Resistance groups transmit essential messages.

Wireless telegraphy operators lived very hazardous lives while serving during the Second World War, but they were also key to Resistance groups being able to function during the war. Without the necessary communications, Resistance strategies would not be coordinated, other agents would not be able to receive warnings, and resources would not be allocated to groups that needed them. Wireless operators were some of the most vulnerable people of those working for the Resistance and Allied forces. While hiding in safe houses, they would string the aerials up in attics or disguise them as washing lines. They tapped out the Morse code on the key of the transmitters. Operators had to wait alone for hours near the transmitter to know if the message had been received. If they remained on the air for more than 20 minutes, the signals could easily be picked up by enemy forces. They needed to move location frequently, carrying the bulky and heavy transmitter with them - which only increased their chances of being detected. In 1943, the life expectancy of a wireless operator was believed to be no more than six weeks.

Before being flown to the location where she would be operating, Khan stayed in a country house in Buckinghamshire. The house was a final place where agents could determine whether or not they felt they were ready to enter the field; here, they adjusted to their new roles and identities, and this was their last chance to reconsider before departure. According to other agents waiting for their departure, Khan became melancholic. This melancholy was partly because she could not tell her mother where she was going or about the nature of her work, and she was overwhelmingly worried about her mother's welfare. A female agent who watched over those in training witnessed Khan's extreme sadness and approached Vera Atkins - the officer in charge of the F Section. The female agent told Atkins that she thought Khan was not ready and should not enter the field. At this time, Khan's brother was also imploring his sister not to go; he believed the dangerous situation would prove difficult for his sister to face while remaining calm. Furthermore, he believed her "deep-rooted pacifist tendencies would prove insurmountable and cause a conflict of faith when faced with such a dangerous and potentially violent situation" (Brain, 2021).

Atkins called Khan back to London to have one last conversation with her; to provide her with an opportunity to back out without any embarrassment or controversy. She refused to be transferred to another area and remained sure that she was ready and willing to enter the field. Khan did, however, ask Atkins not to notify her mother if she went missing; she only wanted her mother to receive bad news if it was absolutely certain that she was dead. Atkins agreed to this, and Khan was ready to be sent off on her first mission. Despite some hesitancy to send her into the field, it had to be done. The SOE did not have enough radio operators in France due to a wave of arrests and compromised networks. It seemed all their efforts were in danger of failing. Despite her incomplete training and doubts about her suitability, Khan was sent to France because of her exceptional skills as a wireless operator and her perfect French. Her idealism fueled her determination to go; she was passionately opposed to forces of occupation - including the British in India.

Unlike the female agents who worked as couriers, Khan did not parachute into France. Instead, she was flown into France on a Lysander in June to a field near Angers. From there, she traveled to Paris to meet with leaders of the Prosper circuit. Khan would operate from Northern France under the cover of a children's nurse named Jeanne-Marie Renier. From then on, Noor Inayat Khan would only be known by her SOE colleagues as 'Madeleine.'

Chapter 8:

The Musician and Writer

Unlike the other female agents whose stories we have already explored, Noor Inayat Khan's time as an agent during the war was over far too soon. The wonderfully creative and talented woman would not see the end of the war and would not be honored in the same way the other female agents were.

A Life Lost Too Soon

Noor Inayat Khan worked for the Prosper network during her time as an operator. Not long after she began to work as a wireless operator in Le Mans, the Gestapo began uncovering Resistance networks (especially those specializing in communication) and began rounding up as many agents as possible. Despite being urged to return to London, Khan decided that she would stay in France. Even while the danger around her was growing, she was determined to stay in France and help liberate the beloved country she grew up in. Khan set up a safe house in Paris and worked as the only transmitting agent in Paris. Khan was only allowed to stay if she agreed not to send any transmissions but only to receive signals; Khan, however, would defy and continue sending transmissions as well.

In order to remain as safe as she could, she moved around frequently and continuously changed her appearance. Her constant change in address and appearance would only keep her safe for about four months. The Gestapo had managed to obtain a description of her and were relentlessly hunting her. They had searched for her for months, and soon their luck would turn. Khan intended to leave Paris and return to England by October 1943; sadly, she would not be able to return to England by her planned date. What is known for sure is that a Frenchwoman betrayed Noor for 100,000 francs; though some sources do not attach an identity to the woman, others believe it was the sister of Henri Garry. Garry was Khan's organizer in the network and head agent of the 'Phono' and 'Cinema' circuits. The betrayal resulted in Khan's capture approximately a day before she planned on returning to England. A French police officer working for the Gestapo had been waiting outside her apartment to capture her. But Khan would not simply give up. Reports made after her death state that she had fought him and only surrendered when he had drawn a gun. Though one might be skeptical, this does not go against Khan's faith; she was determined not to kill another human being during this war, but that did not mean she would willingly walk to her death.

The Gestapo had captured Khan and taken her to their headquarters in Paris. She tried to apply what she had learned in training; Khan attempted to escape twice but was recaptured both times. It was later reported that despite undergoing a grueling interrogation, Khan never gave the Gestapo any information nor revealed anything about her activities. Unfortunately, due to some miscommunication or misunderstanding about filing her messages, Khan kept a copy of every message she sent and received, both in code and decoded. Her notebooks would reveal many things to the German troops. She had become the wireless operator for several circuits in France and had transmitted for many agents in the few months she was there. A memo she made in February 1944 suggested that she had been helping Allied airmen escape after they had been shot down in France. Not only did she have her hands full as a wireless operator, but such was her determination to do good that she had helped wherever she could.

Not only did the Nazis now have access to the codes the SOE was using to communicate with one another, but those in London would not know that Khan had been captured. The Gestapo now had a way of imitating her and continued sending messages to London. Those receiving the messages would not pick up any anomalies and would thus continue sending messages back to Khan. This resulted in agents being sent directly into the hands of the Gestapo; the SOE in London were being deceived, and the incoming agents were being sent to their deaths. Another SOE agent in the area would find out about Khan's arrest and notify those in London to be suspicious of any message sent from 'Madeleine.'

While under arrest, Khan was determined to escape. With the help of two other prisoners, she came up with a plan that might mean their freedom. They loosened bars on their cells and used ripped sheets to climb down the building. Unfortunately, one of the prisoners did not manage to make it very far and, in an attempt to spare his own life, gave up the location of Khan and the third prisoner. Once again in Gestapo custody, Khan was asked if she would promise she would not attempt to escape again. She refused to make that promise.

It was too late for anyone to attempt to save Noor. She was sent to Germany in November 1943. Khan was confined in the Pforzheim prison, kept in chains and placed in solitary confinement; she would be the first British woman to be held in this prison. While in this prison, she was subjected to regular torture sessions, yet she never gave up any information. She was treated as an extremely dangerous prisoner who could not be trusted. Noor would spend the rest of her life in German hands. Despite beatings and constant interrogations, she would never give up any information to the Germans. By scratching her name into bowls, she revealed her true identity to other inmates, along with the address to her mother's home in London.

During her time as a prisoner of war, it is probable that her upbringing in Sufism helped her inwardly. The rite of *dhikr* is a central component of Sufi worship and involves constant, meditative remembrance of God. This rite can be done individually and creates a deeper connection with the divine. Though there are no accounts of Khan partaking in this rite while she was imprisoned, it is possible that she spent time each day strengthening her connection with the divine. In addition, her dedication to her faith, her commitment to remaining free of violence, and her resolution to keep as many people as possible safe, would greatly influence her state of mind.

Khan and three fellow agents were transported to the Dachau concentration camp in September 1944. On the 13th of September 1944, Noor Inayat Khan was executed along with three other female operatives. Throughout her torture and imprisonment, and despite what her brother had feared, she never questioned her faith or wavered in her beliefs. Khan continued to operate under the belief that everyone should have their liberty and freedom defended and that no person or group should be allowed to take away from another, especially not using violent and inhumane tactics. Until her last moment, she was determined to save and protect those she could, even if it meant giving up her own life. This woman of vision and courage was perhaps the bravest of all, because she was not a natural-born fighter and leader of men. She was a courageous idealist who suffered many months of torture and abuse. Nevertheless, she died believing in her principles and paid for them with her life. Her last word before being shot was reported as 'Liberte.' Noor Inayat Khan was a true inspiration and would never forget her ideals, not even at the cost of her own life.

Honored Even Decades Later

Noor Inayat Khan's contributions to the war effort only came to light for the 21st-century world when a biography about her was published in 2008 (*Spy Princess* by Shrabani Basu). After her death, Noor was awarded for her work during the war. Posthumously, she received the George Cross in 1946 and was also awarded the French Croix de Guerre. Basu (2008) mentions: "In France, she is a heroine. They know her as Madeleine of the Resistance, and every year a military band plays outside her childhood home on Bastille Day." In 2012, a statue of Noor was unveiled in the Gordon Square garden where she lived as a child, near her home at 4 Taviton Street. It is the first freestanding memorial for a woman of Asian descent in a public space in Britain and one of the few in the world dedicated to a Muslim woman, a beautiful bronze bust situated in a place she loved. It was unveiled by HRH Princess Anne. At the unveiling, Noor's cousin said, "It was an absolute question of conscience and conviction for her. She could not do otherwise with such a shadow hanging over Europe" (Kennedy, 2012). Noor was the first woman of South Asian descent to receive a blue plaque. In 2020, this plaque was unveiled at her London home that she left behind to undertake her most dangerous mission. Noor Inayat Khan might have been overlooked during and directly after the war, but modern times will not forget her efforts.

Sadly, Noor was one of many women who did not make it out of the war alive. She was sent to France along with 50 other women, and, though the records are not clear, at least 11 of these women died during this time. Noor was only one of many female spies to be killed by the Nazis. But the unique story and tragic death of this creative soul, who refused to kill and always showed kindness and sympathy towards others, can never be forgotten.

Chapter 9:

The Spanish-American Countess – Aline Griffith

Aline Griffith was unlike any of the other female spies whose stories have been explored. She never worked for the SOE; instead, she was solely an OSS agent. Aline Griffith had enough careers and lived through enough adventures that a person unfamiliar with her life would assume the stories all belonged to different people. Her later years were filled with controversy and skepticism, but she remained true to herself and her time as a spy. She certainly made sure her life was as exciting as it could possibly be.

Before Becoming A Countess

Aline Griffith was born in May 1923 in Pearl River, New York. She was the oldest of six children. She was born Maria Aline Griffith Dexter but would go by the name Aline Griffith until her death. Not much is known about her parents or her childhood. There are conflicting thoughts and versions about most details pertaining to Griffith's life; even something as mundane as what her parents did for a living has been disputed. It is believed that her father, William Griffith, was a real estate and insurance broker. Facts about her mother's day-to-day life during her youth are also contradictory. Some say she stayed at home to raise her six children, and others say she was a painter. One detail that remains concrete when it comes to her mother, Marie Dexter, is her claim that she was connected to the Mayflower.

Griffith, a very pretty child, was raised fairly strictly. She was taught that she was to act like a lady from an early age. When the time came, Griffith went to a school near her home; she grew up in a community where everyone was familiar or friendly, so staying near her home for schooling was not uncommon or strange. Griffith attended the College of Mount Saint Vincent and graduated as valedictorian. Griffith graduated with a degree in literature, journalism, and history. She was an incredibly intelligent and attractive young woman.

Once Griffith graduated, she was sought after as a model and eventually decided to work with Hattie Carnegie. She moved to Manhattan to pursue her modeling career. Unfortunately, or perhaps, fortunately, her model career would be cut short. Her younger brothers had all enlisted to help the Allied forces during the Second World War. Griffith was disappointed that she could not aid her country in one way or another. She was 20 years old, and women had to be at least 25 to be hired for a job that could take them overseas. Finally, her luck would turn around at a dinner party, where she escorted a stranger as a favor for a friend.

A Model Recruit

The identity of the man who introduced Griffith to the OSS and the world of espionage is greatly disputed. Some call him Mr. Tomlinson, others refer to him as John Derby, and others know him as Frank Ryan. Regardless of this mystery man's name, Griffith met him at a dinner party, where they struck up a conversation about the political climate in Europe and the ongoing war. This conversation took place in 1943 when Griffith was 20 years old. As mentioned previously, she was of no value to her country; she was not yet old enough to travel to Europe and help on the frontlines. Or so she thought. Griffith revealed to the agent she was distraught that she could not aid the war effort. In a later interview, she mentioned she was furious at dinner; "nobody young wanted to miss something like that at that moment" (Lacher, 1991). The man took great interest in this. Aline Griffith was precisely the type of person the OSS had been looking for. She was a charming, well-spoken, beautiful young woman who would be able to slip into higher society groups with relative ease and gather information the Allied forces so desperately needed. When she, in later years, spoke about the night her recruitment process began, she would relay that "[she] didn't see why these boys should be risking their lives and having the fun of being on the front lines, and girls had to stay home" (Renner, 1987).

He told Griffith he might be able to help her; he could potentially aid her in joining the cause and helping her country. The man told her that he would be in touch if his efforts were successful. At first, Griffith thought nothing of it and refused to get her hopes up. But not long after their first meeting, the man contacted her and gave her an address in Washington where she could go to receive further information. Griffith did not know that the OSS had been carefully going through her credentials to ensure that she would be fit for recruitment and eventual training and deployment.

Nevertheless, with no idea what lay ahead, Griffith traveled to Washington, where she would join the OSS and begin her training. Not much is known or confirmed about the actual recruitment process. It would perhaps be wise to take everything from this point onward with a grain of salt, as one would with any intelligence agent telling their stories. The recruitment process and training time for the OSS was kept hidden, as the OSS, created during the Second World War, was the first of its kind; a formal and legal espionage organization.

Rigorous Training

There are conflicting reports as to the actual location of the OSS training grounds. Some say the training ground was in Maryland; others name the training grounds a private estate near Langley, VA, where the CIA would later be based. What is certain is that the training grounds were referred to as 'The Farm' by OSS members. Training as a spy, or, as Griffith preferred to be called, a 'secret agent', was a relatively new phenomenon in America.

Griffith's training would last three months; she and one other woman trained alongside 30 odd men. The training was tough, but Griffith and her fellow agents would learn valuable skills they would need to survive while in direct contact with enemy forces. Their training began at 07:30 every morning and lasted until midnight each night; the only rest days they had were the occasional weekend off. Griffith learned how to handle and work with a range of firearms and explosives, and she became skilled in hand-to-hand combat. In addition, they were taught how to parachute from planes, how to forge documents that would be essential to their survival, and how to send and receive Morse code. Griffith was one of the very few women who would be invited to join the OSS, and receive and complete the harsh training.

After three months of training that consisted of a grueling schedule designed to test the agents' mental and physical stamina, Griffith was ready for her first mission. She was sent to Spain to discover any enemy forces' plans and to deceive the enemy as much as possible. Griffith stated her main objectives as having to encode and decode messages that passed through the office in Spain and that she had to recruit women for an intelligence network. She would be part of dozens of agents who posed as employees of the American Oil Mission, a company that sold oil to Spain. Griffith would be put in some dangerous situations, but she was more than willing to face these for her country.

Chapter 10:

An OSS Lady Arrives In Spain

Like the other female agents, Aline Griffith faced many more difficulties than her male counterparts, simply because she was a woman. The men she interacted with during her training and her time in Spain could not understand why she would leave the safety of America to enter the dangers of war. But, like with our other spies, being a woman would allow Griffith to accomplish things that her male colleagues were not so easily able to do. Griffith's brief was to uncover enemy secrets; she was to infiltrate Spanish high-society circles and look for signs of Nazi activity.

Adrenaline Filled Missions In Spain

During the Second World War, the neutral countries in Europe proved to be excellent places to conduct espionage. Allied and Axis secret agents flocked to major cities in Spain, Sweden, Portugal, and Switzerland. In the early months of 1944, Aline Griffith arrived in Madrid, Spain, to begin her life of espionage. Though it could not be known at the time, the war was nearing its end, and Griffith would be overly prepared for a battle she would never have to fight in. Her codename was 'Tiger;' appropriate for the fierce and eye-catching woman entering the war zone.

A Redacted Mission Brief

In 1944, when she was only 21 years old, Griffith played a crucial role in a mission that would ensure the safety of thousands of Allied troops as they prepared to liberate occupied territories in Europe. 'Operation Anvil' was focused on the planned invasion of southern France in 1944. A fact that counted both in her favor, and against her, as well, is that she was not given much information regarding the operation. Griffith knew she would be helping other agents execute the plan, but she did not know exactly how she was going to help. She was used as bait to fool a double agent; only Griffith had no idea the man was acting as a double agent for the Germans. The agent was known as Pierre and had trained with Griffith; she believed him to be genuine, so she showed a true sense of affection towards him. The information she gave him would be highly believable - she did not know it was false, and their amicable relationship meant he had no reason not to believe her.

Griffith would not know the full extent of her role in this operation until it was officially over. She would learn that Pierre remained part of the OSS *because* he was a double agent. From the very start, the OSS had known that he was loyal to the Nazis and had used him, and later the unsuspecting Griffith, to funnel false information to the German troops. The false information would lead to the German forces preparing for an Allied invasion at a location, date, and time that was not accurate. Griffith began to suspect her true role in Operation Anvil when she heard a message being transmitted over the radio; the message mentioned that 94,000 Allied troops had arrived near a fishing village in Saint-Tropez. The information Griffith received and gave Pierre was that the troops would land in and invade Marseilles - over 62 miles from where the troops actually landed.

After the invasion proved successful, her OSS handler in Madrid (a man code-named Mozart) told her the truth about the operation she was a part of. He explained to her that without her help, they would have had to count their losses and could not consider the Allied landing to be a victory. Given the nature of the task, it is unlikely that a man would have been able to accomplish what Griffith successfully managed to do. Without her help, thousands of troops would have been killed by German forces, and France would not have been liberated.

Narrowly Avoiding Death

Like many other secret agents, Griffith faced her fair share of dangerous situations and near-death experiences. However, she was in a somewhat safer situation than those in the thick of the action in France. Her goal was to gather information from high-ranking Nazi officials and socialites that could provide the Allied forces with valuable information. But during her time in Spain, there was one experience that brought her much closer to death than she would have liked to be.

Griffith was instructed to infiltrate high-society circles and parties where she could glean intelligence from gossip and information shared between officials who frequented these spaces. At one of these glittering occasions, she was to face a level of danger she had not yet been exposed to since arriving in Madrid.

Griffith had been attending a ball in 1944 at a Madrid country club, Puerta de Hierro. As she was leaving the ball, a double agent found an excuse not to take her back to their lodgings, but instead convinced her to get into a car with a specific driver. Griffith had no idea that the agent she had trusted, because they worked together, was a mole. Once in the car, shortly after departing from the country club, the driver attempted to kill her. He pulled over to the side of the road, but as soon as the car stopped, Griffith jumped out. She began running away, a wondrous feat as she was wearing high heels at the time, and he ran after her in pursuit. He grabbed her and attempted to strangle her with the full intent of killing her.

Griffith, luckily, had been carrying a gun with her in her purse. She pulled the gun out and managed to shoot him during their scuffle. Griffith stated that the driver had gone limp and fallen on top of her. She assumed, but was not certain, that she had shot and killed him. In her haste to leave the scene, she had not stopped to take his pulse. The following day, her bosses confused Griffith even further; they told her that she had killed him but then changed their story. Today, however, it is widely accepted that Griffith indeed managed to kill the man who attacked her.

Constant Danger

During her time in Madrid working for the OSS, there was rarely a moment where she did not face danger or the risk of being exposed. The ever-present danger was evident to Griffith after her first night in Madrid. She had gone out for a late dinner and then attended a performance of flamenco dance; it seemed like a relatively safe thing to do as a young woman in a new country. But the following day, she was visited by the employees of a great matador, who wanted to pay respects on behalf of their employer and ask her out on a date with him! This unexpected visit proved that she would not be able to fly underneath the radar, as she had hoped. Griffith had thought that her comings and goings were supposed to be kept under wraps, but this incident revealed that anonymity was hard to come by and secrets were hard to keep, especially if the secrets held a high value.

Madrid was a wonderful place with an exciting nightlife. However, along with the sophisticated atmosphere, Madrid was also full of German spies and double agents and was a perilous place in which to operate. She quickly learned that moving in high-society circles was a fine way of gathering the information that would aid the Allied cause. As she later explained, "Because I was a girl and because I was so young, no one suspected I would be doing something so important or so dangerous" (Renner, 1987). Griffith made sure she was a prominent fixture in the local social life; those she socialized with would believe they could trust her and, as a result, shared their secrets with her. She regularly attended the opera and dined at fine restaurants. Almost every weekend, she would be invited to spend time at some nobleman's country estate. Using the money she received from the OSS, she bought expensive Balenciaga dresses that allowed her to fit into the high-society crowd as if born to it. This was all a cover and allowed her to reach the objectives set out for her before she embarked on her mission. For a former high-life fashion model, this assignment seemed not only tailor-made, but fun!

Griffith soon had many admirers among the people she mingled with. She got to know European royalty and quickly became a fashion icon while in the presence of these royals. Her college education had further sharpened her quick and analytical mind. Griffith was highly adept at sifting through all the gossip she heard to find meaningful intelligence she could present to her handlers, often leaving them extremely impressed. Aline Griffith knew how to use her wit, charm, and beauty to get secrets from officials and high-ranking men. She was constantly surrounded by high-ranking officials on the other side of the war. Griffith was frequently presented with opportunities to gather information on those she was fighting against. At one mansion she had been invited to, she managed to get a look inside their guest book and was able to look for the names of Nazis. During a night out at an exclusive nightclub, she caught a glimpse of SS leader Heinrich Himmler in a private room and could inform her bosses that the SS head was secretly working in Spain.

Griffith was in constant danger, especially because she was regularly close to these officials. OSS agents did not have diplomatic immunity, and espionage was a capital crime at the time. She was jailed for a brief period of time in Malaga because she was traveling without the proper and necessary papers. The arrest had almost blown her cover, and because she had been carrying a list of safe houses to give to another agent, other agents could have been endangered as well.

While operating in Madrid, Griffith recruited local women to work as agents. She provided a safe haven for two Spanish female agents on the run. The women stayed at her apartment in Madrid while she was away for a weekend, looking for a German radio station. When Griffith returned, she discovered that one of the women had been shot and killed in her bed. It is unclear whether the assailant knew that the woman in the bed was not Griffith, or if the killer's intended victim was actually the tenant of the house because he knew she was a spy!

Griffith's handler, Mozart, also constantly reminded her how to ensure she would not give up any valuable information. He encouraged her to use the lethal "L pill' if she was ever captured. Biting on this would result in her death, to prevent her accidentally betraying the OSS during torture. All agents carried lethal pills to avoid capture and torture; no one wanted to betray their colleagues under the duress of torture. In February 1945, she would be involved in a more dangerous assignment than she had been thus far. The United States government had become very concerned about the wealth Nazi officials carried through Spain while on their way to safe havens. Griffith's job was to identify those involved and uncover how they moved the money.

The operation continued even after the war ended, as Nazi officials were attempting to escape prosecution, and most went into hiding. As the war was nearing its end, Griffith's bosses gave her two options for her future; she could quit the espionage business now, or she could wait for them to assemble the CIA. If she chose to continue with her espionage career, she would be sent to Switzerland on her first mission for the CIA.

Life In Spain After The War

After her career as a secret agent ended, Aline Griffith stated, "Espionage becomes like a drug. It makes life very exciting. You know things other people don't know—you're always going under the surface. I was trained as a spy very early, and it became a part of me. I got accustomed to living with a certain amount of tension" (Harvey, 2018). Like most involved in the life of espionage, Griffith would have trouble adjusting after the war; she used to carry a gun and suicide pills in her purse wherever she went, even though she no longer needed them.

Aline Griffith stayed in Spain after the war had ended and continued sending the information she gathered to her bosses. She never received any awards or honors for her time as an OSS agent, but that did not seem too important to her. A moment during the war would determine the choices Griffith would make regarding her future. While working undercover as a socialite in Madrid's high-society circles, she met her future husband. Luis Figueroa y Pérez de Guzmán El Bueno was, at that time, the Count of Quintanilla, and would later become the Count of Romanones. Griffith did not have to worry about whether or not Luis was working for the Germans; he was very much pro-American. The couple got along very well, but neither knew what they were getting themselves into. She had no idea just how wealthy her future husband was. He was driving a car that was almost 10 years old, one of the few vintage vehicles to be seen during wartime in Spain. It would only be later, during their marriage, that she discovered more about the extent of his riches - she would find out that her husband owned a castle and would eagerly want to restore it to live there (she even wrote her first book about the castle). Years later, Griffith recalled that she never expected to marry a Spaniard, no less a grandee of Spain, when she began her work in Spain. And she had no idea that she would spend the rest of her life calling the country her home.

Around the time her bosses were waiting for an answer regarding her decision about the CIA, Luis proposed, and Griffith's mind was made up. For the time being, she would stop her work as a spy and pursue the family life she wanted. When they got engaged, Griffith told Luis that she was a spy and worked for the OSS. He did not believe her; instead, Luis laughed and complimented her on her vivid and creative imagination. However, he also warned her that her 'fantasy stories' would do nothing to improve her future in-laws' opinion of her, and to stay quiet on the subject. So, she decided she would not press the issue and allowed her future husband to believe what he pleased.

Only years later, when they met one of Griffith's old bosses, her husband realized that she had been telling the truth before their marriage. Some say it was due to him that she left the world of espionage. Luis had asked her to quit so she would not be in unnecessary danger. Her fiancé's disbelief that she could have been a secret agent simply proves that men had always underestimated her. When she was recruited during her time in Madrid, Aline Griffith was always underestimated because of her beauty and youth. But she was never afraid of proving people wrong.

For the first five or six years of her marriage, she had no involvement in any espionage activities. In 1947, Griffith married the Count of Romanones and became the Countess of Romanones. The Count and Countess had three sons during that time (and she would later be a grandmother to 13 grandchildren). Then, about a decade after the end of the Second World War, Griffith received a call from an old colleague in Washington. The CIA wanted to know if she was willing to do the occasional odd job for them. It would involve traveling, which is something she always enjoyed. For Griffith, the only logical choice would be to agree.

During her relationship with Luis, and even more so during their marriage, she formed relationships with many important people, not only in Spain but also in other countries. The CIA felt that her high-profile contacts would be a great asset. Griffith could once again gather information for the organization by simply living lavishly and being herself. She could very easily travel around the world and do the small jobs the CIA required of her. She mingled with first ladies, artists, actors, other aristocrats, and important politicians and officials as a countess. As had been the case during the war, she was the perfect person to gather the needed intelligence. No one would suspect a woman such as herself of being a spy; there were no spies in the social circles she found herself in. The details of her missions during this time have not been made known or available to the public

But the life of an essential and valuable spy was not enough for Aline Griffith. She loved her life of wealth and glamor and wanted more of that. Griffith wanted to be known, not only for her work as a spy (though she knew she might never be recognized for that) but for her life after her espionage career came to a close. Today, she is known as an actor and writer. In the world of acting and television, Griffith is most known for Late Night with David Letterman (1982), Angel Casos Show (1984), and Garbo: The Spy (2009). In this world, she was surrounded by high-profile people, something she had become accustomed to during her youth. After the war, some of her greatest friends were people from the higher society; the Duke and Duchess of Windsor and Audrey Hepburn and her husband, Mel Ferrer.

Perhaps Griffith's most well-known and most controversial career choice has been that of a writer. In 1986, Aline Griffith published her first book. It was a slightly embellished and fictionalized memoir about her time as a spy. Nevertheless, the memoirs served as an insight into the thoughts and feelings of a young, adventurous woman who was eager to play an active role in World War II. She wrote two more books and was heavily criticized by those who had some knowledge of the world of intelligence agencies and espionage. In total, Griffith wrote six books about espionage during her lifetime. Three books, 'The Spy…' series, were explicitly dedicated to her time as a secret agent during and after the Second World War. The books in the memoir series were titled *The Spy Wore Red* (1987), *The Spy Went Dancing* (1990), and *The Spy Wore Silk* (1991). Her other books were titled, *The Story of Pascualete/The Earth Rests Lightly* (1963), *An American in Spain* (1980), and *The Well-Mannered Assassin* (1994).

On more than one occasion, Griffith was accused of writing anecdotes that were entirely made up. Or, as was often stated, she changed the stories of some missions and reports into something more dangerous and adventurous than they were. She received especially heavy criticism for writing about her part in aiding the capture of a mole within the CIA. Other agents and journalists seemed to believe that Griffith was taking credit for the discovery and arrest of the mole when it had taken over two years and 200 people to flush out the double-agent. Griffith stated that she did not at all pretend to do it single-handedly. She simply wrote about the CIA approaching her to help them find the mole in their midst.

In 1991, she faced great controversy in New York because of her books. Many believed that her memoirs were simply fictitious stories told to make her life seem more extraordinary than it was. Reporters claimed that she never had an encounter with a driver attempting to kill her and that she never aided the Allied troops' arrival by working on Operation Anvil. Griffith passionately defended her books. She said it would be impossible for the details of her missions in Spain to be kept on file; she had no reason to lie about her life during the war.

Sometime after the death of her husband in 1987, she commented that, until then, she had not yet shaken the feeling of immortality left in a person who has frequently put their life on the line and survived. Griffith said that the constant danger of the life of a spy often made them believe that life would continue without end. The loss of her husband was a sobering reminder of her mortality and how easily her life could slip away from her.

Griffith eventually returned to the United States. At one stage, she spent the majority of the year in a one-bedroom apartment in New York City, where she wrote, and bought and sold sheep for her ranch in Spain by telephone. Aline Griffith passed away in 2017 on December 11, in Madrid, where her adventurous life had truly begun. Of the five female agents discussed, Aline Griffith was the youngest to join the effort and the one whose life was most filled with high-rollers and glittering nights out.

Conclusion

As we look back on the incredible lives of these five women, we cannot help but marvel at their courage, and that of the many other women spies in WWII whose stories have yet to be told. We can wonder if they knew of one another and if their paths ever crossed during the war. Of course, all secret agents had taken an oath of confidentiality and were unable to speak of their experiences until records had been declassified, but what would it have been like if they had all survived to meet in later life? A picture emerges of an imaginary scene: a comfortable hotel lounge in which five brave older women are being served afternoon tea. Virginia Hall and Aline Griffith would exchange tales of the excitement of embarking on their journeys from America to Europe. Nancy Wake, who left behind her poverty-stricken past in Australia, would understand their desire to seek new horizons far from their countries of origin. Christine Granville would confess her pain at being rejected as a rebel; neither fitting into the society of her birth nor ever finding a sense of belonging anywhere else, always hungry for adventure. Virginia and Nancy would surely have raised a few eyebrows, discussing their experiences as female leaders in charge of bands of men, the Maquis Resistance fighters – some friendly, some extremely hostile - hiding in the forests. They could all have shared a wry smile, comparing notes at the many times their authority was undermined by their male colleagues. Noor Inayat Khan would show her published writings to Nancy, who would reminisce about her time as a journalist before marrying into high society and entering the war zone. If Noor had survived, perhaps she would have written a haunting and compelling tale, weaving together the common threads of these women's stories. In our imagined scene, these courageous female spies could have become close friends and confidantes; sharing, at last, the pain, fear, loneliness and distrust they experienced during their work in the field and how their achievements came at a great personal cost. Together they would have grieved the loss of comrades and loved ones. They had much in common; they put their lives on the line for their belief in an ideal of freedom. Finally, all of them would clearly see the path they had created for future women to excel in their chosen fields.

In the 21st century Western world, women are no longer second-class citizens who are excluded from certain careers reserved only for men. The Women's Rights Movement worked to ensure better lives and futures for all women, who have found places of leadership and positions of power in several fields. Women now have far more opportunities for careers, education, and travel. There is no doubt that women still face sexism, they are still excluded from certain circles, they often still have to prove themselves by being better than anyone else in order to be taken seriously. But unlike our women heroes of WWII, perhaps they are no longer considered as a last-resort option for posts only when there are insufficient trained men available. Women now have far greater opportunities to serve in military positions in many nations. Young girls have more role models than ever to look up to - the agents profiled in the book are an example of this.

Some lessons can be learned from these five exceptional women. They were willing to put their lives in danger for countries that were not their own, or for countries that later shunned them. They did this despite being looked down upon and having their competence doubted. Throughout the course of their service as agents in the world of secret intelligence, these women were doubted and belittled. They faced great prejudice in a world made for men by men. But despite all these obstacles, they moved forward and became some of the best and most highly valued agents to come to the Allied forces' aid during the Second World War.

These five female agents, and many others whose stories have yet to be told, were trailblazers. They created opportunities and opened doors for many generations of women that would come after them. Never once did they waver in the face of the enemy; never once did they back down, even when they were unsure that they would emerge victoriously. Some of their missions and achievements held more danger than faced by their male counterparts during the Second World War. Misogyny was widespread, both within Nazi ideology and, sadly, their own intelligence organizations. Both sides were blinded by their ideas of what a woman can and cannot do; both sides underestimated how powerful women can be in the face of war. It is sad that due to the secret nature of their work and the oaths of silence they were bound by, they could not claim honor or reminisce on their time during the war like other veterans could. They were not celebrated in annual veterans' rallies. They were always left behind. If one thing stands out from the studying the lives of these women, it is this; nothing should stand in the way of the defense of one's principles and values. No obstacle was too significant to face in their determination to dedicate their lives to liberating others from the forces of oppression. These female agents overcame great difficulties, faced much prejudice, and are now forever remembered as some of the most extraordinary people to fight during the Second World War. Virginia Hall, Christine Granville, Nancy Wake, Noor Inayat Khan, and Aline Griffith deserve to be remembered for the brave and fierce intelligence agents they were. And perhaps, once you have turned the last page and closed this book, you will go out and tell others about these incredible women and keep their legacy alive until the end of time.

About The Author

Elise Baker's academic background (BA Hons, PGDip) and a career of searching for hidden truths in dusty libraries and archives led her to discover an area of history that has languished in obscurity for far too long; the women heroes of WW2, whose achievements have long been overshadowed by their male counterparts, silenced and rendered invisible by the secret nature of their work and their gender.

Her mother's family spent years wandering around Europe as refugees during the Second World War and its aftermath. Growing up hearing their stories gave her a lifelong fascination with this historical era.

She has a special interest in feminism, women's history, and World War II. Elise is passionate about excavating the past to unearth the hidden histories of women whose incredible stories have been buried and bringing them out into the light of public awareness.

If you have enjoyed reading this book, it would be greatly appreciated if you would be so kind as to take a moment to leave a review. For more books in the Brave Women Who Changed the Course of World War II Series please visit: **www.elise-baker.com**

Glossary

Abwher: An organization that was responsible for gathering military intelligence for Germany from 1921 to 1944.

Allied Forces: A military coalition formed during World War II to oppose the Axis powers; Great Britain, the United States, and the Soviet Union.

Axis Powers: A military coalition that initiated the Second World War; Germany, Japan, and Italy.

CBE: Commander of the Order of the British Empire

CIA: Central Intelligence Agency

Concentration Camp: A place where a large number of people, usually minorities or political enemies, are imprisoned without proper care and forced to either provide labor or wait for mass execution.

Courier: A person employed to carry intelligence for an espionage organization.

Croix de Guerre: A military decoration in France.

Diplomat: Someone skilled or employed in diplomacy.

George Medal: A decoration of the United Kingdom and Commonwealth, awarded for acts of great bravery.

Gestapo: German secret state police; the political police of Nazi Germany

Intelligence: Knowledge concerning events obtained from someone else; information that holds military value.

Intelligence Agency: An agency for obtaining information of military or political value; for espionage.

Internment Camp: A prison camp where prisoners of war, political prisoners, or enemies are confined.

MBE: Member of the Order of the British Empire

Maquis: A French resistance movement active during the German occupation in the Second World War.

Nazi(s): A Member/Members of the National Socialist German Workers' Party.

OBE: The Order of the British Empire

OSS: Office of Strategic Services (American)

Resistance: A secret organization that resists authority in an occupied country.

SOE: Special Operations Executive (British)

WAAF: Women's Auxiliary Air Force

Wireless Operator: A person who operates a radio transmitter for a military unit to communicate over long distances.

References

If you feel inspired to learn more about the lives of these noteworthy agents, there are several in-depth biographies to read. In *A Woman of No Importance* (2019), Sonia Purnell dives deeper into the challenges faced by Virginia Hall. Claire Mulley brings readers to tears in *The Spy Who Loved* (2012) with Christine Granville's story. The colorful character of Nancy Wake is brought to life in Russell Braddon's *Nancy Wake: World War Two's Most Rebellious Spy* (2019, revised and first published 1956). Noor Inayat Khan lives on in the hearts of many in *Spy Princess: The Life of Noor Inayat Khan* (2008) by Shrabani Basu. Aline Griffith remains glamorous and daring in Larry Loftis' *The Princess Spy: The True Story of World War II Spy Aline Griffith, Countess of Romanones* (2021).

Atwood, K. J. (2019). *Women heroes of World War II: 32 stories of espionage, sabotage, resistance, and rescue.* Chicago Review.

Australian War Memorial. (2011). *Nancy Grace Augusta "The White Mouse" Wake.* Awm.gov.au. https://www.awm.gov.au/collection/P332

BBC. (2014). *BBC - History - Noor Inayat Khan.* Bbc.co.uk. https://www.bbc.co.uk/history/historic_figures/inayat_khan_noor.shtml

Shrabani Basu. (2008). *Spy princess : the life of Noor Inayat Khan.* The History Press.

Brain, J. (2021, September 16). *The Bravery of Noor Inayat Khan.* Historic UK https://www.historicuk.com/HistoryUK/HistoryofBritain/Bravery-Of-Noor-Inayat-Khan/

Braddon, R. (2019, prev. published 1956). *Nancy Wake: World War Two's Most Rebellious Spy*, Little A.

Central Intelligence Agency. (2017, June 30). *Virginia Hall:The Courage and Daring of "The Limping Lady"* - CIA. Www.cia.gov. https://www.cia.gov/stories/story/virginia-hall-the-courage-and-daring-of-the-limping-lady/

Conroy, S. B. (1991, April 27). *THE SPY'S NEW CLOTHES*. Washington Post. https://www.washingtonpost.com/archive/lifestyle/1991/04/27/the-spys-new-clothes/f11c221e-bfb7-4e05-8574-e736c43c8ec0/

Cutler, J. (2021, February 5). *What a wild life: New York woman's rise from model to spy to countess.* Nydailynews.com. https://www.nydailynews.com/entertainment/ny-princess-spy-book-20210205-3go3bedsz5hrjo4m7e4ue5wcne-story.html

Eder, M. K. (2022). *The Girls Who Stepped Out of Line: Untold Stories of the Women Who Changed the Course of World War II.* Sourcebooks Inc.

Elder, G. (2016, October 27). *Faces of Defense Intelligence: Virginia Hall - The "Limping Lady."* Defense Intelligence Agency. https://www.dia.mil/News-Features/Articles/Article-View/Article/988284/faces-of-defense-intelligence-virginia-hall-the-limping-lady/

Encyclopedia of World Biography. (n.d.). *Christine Granville Biography - life, childhood, name, story, death, wife, school, mother, young.* www.notablebiographies.com. https://www.notablebiographies.com/supp/Supplement-Fl-Ka/Granville-Christine.html

Escott, Beryl. (2010). *The Heroines of SOE: F Section, Britain's Secret Women in France.* The History Press

Harvey, I. (2018, January 26). *The Countess of Romanones, María Aline Griffith, "The Countess Spy" Dies at 94.* WAR HISTORY ONLINE. https://www.warhistoryonline.com/featured/the-countess-of-romanones.html?chrome=1

Independent.ie. (2011, August 11). *Nancy Wake*. Independent. https://www.independent.ie/world-news/nancy-wake-26761178.html

Jewish Virtual Library. (2011). *Nancy Wake*. Jewishvirtuallibrary.org. https://www.jewishvirtuallibrary.org/nancy-wake

Kealey, I. (2020, April 28). *Meet Nancy Wake: Socialite, Spy, and The Most Decorated Heroine of WWII*. CrimeReads. https://crimereads.com/meet-nancy-wake-socialite-spy-and-the-most-decorated-heroine-of-wwii/

Kennedy, M. (2012, November 8). *Statue honours Indian secret agent killed at concentration camp*. The Guardian. https://www.theguardian.com/world/2012/nov/08/statue-indian-secret-agent-killed

Lacher, I. (1991, March 10). *A Woman of Mystery : Espionage: Countess Aline Romanones has written no less than three books about her exploits as a spy. But* skeptics keep asking: Is she all she says she is? Los Angeles Times. https://www.latimes.com/archives/la-xpm-1991-03-10-vw-55-story.html

Loftis, L. (2021). *The Princess Spy: The True Story of World War II Spy Aline Griffith, Countess of Romanones*. Atria Books.

Martin, C. (1999, April 2). *THE LEISURELY PACE OF AN ELEGANT SPY*. Chicago Tribune. https://www.chicagotribune.com/news/ct-xpm-1991-04-02-9101300354-story.html

Matters, M. H. (2018, May 11). *Krystyna Skarbek: the SOE's silent killer |* Military History Matters. Www.military-History.org. https://www.military-history.org/feature/krystyna-skarbek-the-soes-silent-killer.htm

Mauzac Prison Break. (2019, November 20). Rhap.so.dy in Words. https://rhapsodyinwords.com/tag/mauzac-prison-break/

Mulley, C. (2014). *The spy who loved : the secrets and lives of Christine Granville*. St. Martin's Griffin.

Nambi, K. (2020, June 29). *Gestapo's Most Wanted person in World War II - Nancy Wake*. Medium. https://medium.com/lessons-from-history/gestapos-most-wanted-person-in-world-war-ii-nancy-wake-68e84701ca06

Nast, C. (2020, October 30). *The remarkable story of the Muslim Princess who spied for the British during World War II*. Tatler. https://www.tatler.com/article/noor-inayat-khan-muslim-spy-princess-a-call-to-spy

Purnell, S. (2019, April 9). *Virginia Hall Was America's Most Successful Female WWII Spy. But She Was Almost Kept From Serving*. Time. https://time.com/5566062/virginia-hall/

Purnell, S. (2020). *WOMAN OF NO IMPORTANCE : the Untold Story of WWII's Most Dangerous Spy, Virginia Hall*. Virago Press Ltd.

Renner, L. (1987, July 2). *I SPIED: MEMORIES OF THE LADY IN RED*. Orlando Sentinel. https://www.orlandosentinel.com/news/os-xpm-1987-07-02-0180120018-story.html

Rose, S. (2019) *D-Day Girls: The Spies Who Armed the Resistance, Sabotaged the Nazis, and Helped Win the Second World War*. Sphere.

Schimmel, A. (2018). *Sufism | Islam*. In Encyclopædia Britannica. https://www.britannica.com/topic/Sufism

Siddiqui, U. (2020, October 28). *Noor Inayat Khan: The forgotten Muslim princess who fought Nazis*. www.aljazeera.com. https://www.aljazeera.com/features/2020/10/28/noor-inayat-khan

Simkin, J. (2011). *Nancy Wake*. Spartacus Educational. https://spartacus-educational.com/SOEwake.htm

Tsang, A. (2018, November 28). *Overlooked No More: Noor Inayat Khan, Indian Princess and British Spy.* The New York Times. https://www.nytimes.com/2018/11/28/obituaries/ noor-inayat-khan-overlooked.html

Vigurs, K. (2021) Mission France: The True History of the Women of SOE. Yale University Press.

Warwick, M., & Nonfiction | 0. (2021, March 24). *The American fashion model who spied for the Allies in World War II.* Mal Warwick on Books. https://malwarwickonbooks.com/oss-spy/

Wikipedia Contributors. (2019a, February 27). *Noor Inayat Khan.* Wikipedia; Wikimedia Foundation. https://en.wikipedia.org/wiki/Noor_Inayat_Khan

Wikipedia Contributors. (2019b, March 28). *Nancy Wake.* Wikipedia; Wikimedia Foundation. https://en.wikipedia.org/wiki/Nancy_Wake

Wikipedia Contributors. (2019c, November 3). *Virginia Hall.* Wikipedia; Wikimedia Foundation. https://en.wikipedia.org/wiki/Virginia_Hall

Wikipedia Contributors. (2021a, October 2). *Krystyna Skarbek.* Wikipedia. https://en.wikipedia.org/wiki/Krystyna_Skarbek

Wikipedia Contributors. (2021b, December 31). *Aline Griffith,* Countess of Romanones. Wikipedia. https://en.wikipedia.org/wiki/Aline_Griffith

Images

Australian War Memorial (1945). [Figure 3: Studio Portrait of
   Nancy Wake, 1945, Photograph P00885.001].
   https://www.awm.gov.au/collection/P332

Bornhorst, M. (2020c, November 5). Photo by Matthew Bornhorst
   on Unsplash. Unsplash.com.
   https://unsplash.com/photos/YV4dPipE91U

Burke, T. (2019, March 2). Dachau (preserved) concentration camp,
   Dachau, Germany. Unsplash.com.
   https://unsplash.com/photos/4Kr-HCx-Y6c

CIA People. (1945). [Figure 1: Virginia Hall, 1945].
   https://upload.wikimedia.org/wikipedia/commons/1/11/
   Virginia_Hall.jpg CIA People
   (https://commons.wikimedia.org/wiki/File:Virginia_Hall.jpg),
   "Virginia Hall", marked as public domain, more details
   on Wikimedia Commons:
   https://commons.wikimedia.org/wiki/Template:PD-US

Imperial War Museum. (1944). [Figure 2: Krystyna Skarbek, 1944]
   ©Imperial War Museum (HU 47952)

Imperial War Museum. (1944). [Figure 4: Noor Inayat Khan, 1942]
   ©Imperial War Museum (HU 74868)

Redman, J. (2021, February 14). Photo by Johen Redman on
   Unsplash. Unsplash.com.
   https://unsplash.com/photos/i9apY-5hNEw

Other Books by Elise Baker

Women Code Breakers: The Best Kept Secret of WWII
True Stories of Female Code Breakers Whose Top-Secret Work Helped Win WWII

Nightingales, Bluebirds and Angels of Mercy
True Stories of the Courage and Heroism of Nurses on the Frontlines in WWII

Women Rescuers of WWII
True stories of the unsung women heroes who rescued refugees and Allied servicemen in WWII

Ingram Content Group UK Ltd.
Milton Keynes UK
UKHW040713120723
424996UK00001B/91